WHAT PHILOSOPHY CAN DO

LANGUAGE AND THE PURSUIT OF TRUTH
THINKING WITH CONCEPTS
REASON AND MORALS
PHILOSOPHY AND RELIGION
PHILOSOPHY
EDUCATION IN RELIGION AND THE EMOTIONS
PRACTICAL METHODS OF MORAL EDUCATION
RELIGION
INTRODUCTION TO MORAL EDUCATION
LOGIC AND SEXUAL MORALITY
THE CONCEPT OF MENTAL HEALTH
PHILOSOPHY AND PRACTICAL EDUCATION
PREFACE TO THE PHILOSOPHY OF EDUCATION
LANGUAGE AND CHRISTIAN BELIEF
THE TRUTH OF RELIGION
EQUALITY
A TEACHER'S GUIDE TO MORAL EDUCATION
LOVE, SEX AND MORALITY
FANTASY AND COMMON SENSE IN EDUCATION
PUBLIC SCHOOLS AND PRIVATE PRACTICE
PHILOSOPHY AND EDUCATIONAL RESEARCH
EDUCATIONAL THEORY AND THE PREPARATION OF
TEACHERS
THE ASSESSMENT OF MORALITY
DISCIPLINE AND MORAL EDUCATION
MORAL EDUCATION AND THE CURRICULUM
PYLOS 425
ATHENS AND CORCYRA
CANOEING DOWN THE RHÔNE
THE FAITH OF AN ARTIST (*editor*)

WHAT PHILOSOPHY CAN DO

John Wilson

BARNES & NOBLE BOOKS
TOTOWA, NEW JERSEY

First published in the USA 1986 *by*
BARNES & NOBLE BOOKS
81 ADAMS DRIVE
TOTOWA, NEW JERSEY 07512

Printed in Hong Kong

Library of Congress Cataloging-in-Publication Data
Wilson, John, 1928–
What philosophy can do.
Includes index.
1. Philosophy. 2. Methodology. I. Title.
B72.W55   1986   101   86–3413
ISBN 0–389–20622–9
ISBN 0–389–20623–7 (pbk.)

Contents

Preface   vii

Introduction   1

1   Mistakes about Conceptual Analysis   14

2   Concepts and Contestability   41

3   Conceptual Necessity   60

4   Two Examples   81

5   Reactions to Philosophy   102

6   Reactions to Reason   132

A Practical Postscript   151

References   154

Suggestions for Introductory Reading   156

Index   158

Preface

In this book I try to describe, as clearly and simply as I can, (1) the nature and powers of philosophy (or a certain kind of philosophy), and (2) some of the main problems about teaching and learning it. Anyone whose chief interest and experience lie, as mine do, at the interface between philosophy and its practical applications is obliged to look in both of the directions represented by (1) and (2); and in neither direction is the view particularly encouraging. Very little has been written about (1) the nature and powers of philosophy: certainly there is no agreed set of doctrines at the present time (if there ever was) which can be taken down ready-made, as it were, from the shelves of authoritative philosophers. As for (2) – the way in which philosophy is or ought to be presented, and the way in which it is or ought to be received – virtually nothing worth reading has been written at all.

In face of these great difficulties I can only plead that the topic must surely be of equally great importance: particularly, perhaps, in these days of widespread uncertainty. As the immense diversity of practice (even in the same institution) shows, teachers and students of philosophy in universities and other academic settings are often very much in doubt about what to do under that heading; and for many decades now the layman, in English-speaking countries and (for other reasons) elsewhere, has been denied any clear idea either about the nature of philosophy or about its relevance to his practical life. The net result, I suspect, has been to make people more and more doubtful and bewildered about philosophy, often to the point of despair: they are apt to write off philosophy as a bad job, and take up some kind of ideological commitment instead.

I do not feel guilty about having a particular view of philosophy: I shall try to show the reader why it is the right view, and there are already plenty of books which give a general conspectus of different kinds of philosophical or ideological schools and movements – something I shall not attempt here. More worrying is the fact that I am very well aware of touching, here and there, on philosophical problems which are both extremely difficult and much debated by many able philosophers. In a general book of this kind there is no help for that, and no entirely satisfactory way of proceeding: naivety is bound to show. Professional philosophers may well regard much of what I have to say as either wrong or obvious (a common Morton's Fork in philosophical criticism): I do not much mind the latter, pleading only that the obvious in this case is not widely understood or accepted; and where I am wrong, I hope at least to have stimulated other writers to give a more satisfactory account.

J. B. W.

Oxford

Introduction

Most people think, and have always thought, that philosophy ought to tell us at least two sorts of things: (1) what is permanently and universally true and real, or what certain very general and very important features of the world are like; and (2) what is permanently and universally valuable and desirable, or what it is to live well. I say 'permanently and universally', because few people now expect philosophers as such to tell them about what is of only temporary or local importance or desirability, about what is relevant only to certain people in certain situations: these matters are for those who wield the more practical arts and sciences – economists, scientists, doctors, and so on. Some of these specialisms are of comparatively recent growth, and in the past people had still wider expectations of philosophy; but even today, and even in the most technologically advanced societies, philosophy is commonly expected to undertake these two tasks.

It is (I shall argue) entirely right and proper that people should think thus. But the actual practice and – what may, for the layman, carry even greater weight – the presentation of philosophy may well make them despair. They are presented, on the one hand, with various enterprises which do indeed aim, or appear to aim, at telling them these things; and some at least of these are commonly called 'philosophy' or 'philosophies' ('philosophies of life', such as Marxism) even if others might better be described as religions or ideologies. But the trouble with these is – however much or little people are in fact troubled – that they are not in any very obvious way based on the solid grounds of public reason. For some people, at least, want not just to be *told*, but to have *proved* to them beyond reasonable doubt, what certain central realities in the world are, and how they ought to live; and it is not clear, though to a person committed to one of them it may seem clear, that any 'philosophy' or ideology of this sort has succeeded in the task.

1

On the other hand, they are presented with the writings and discourse of some academic philosophers – including, in most English-speaking countries, those who have been called 'conceptual analysts': and these, though apparently concerned to establish things by reason rather than sell them by propaganda or non-rational persuasion, are not very obviously in the twin businesses of saying what the world is like and how we ought to live. People are thus confined, or so it appears to them, either to the option of taking up some 'philosophy of life' without worrying too much about whether it is reasonable, or to the equally unwelcome option of taking up professional philosophy without worrying too much about whether (as people commonly say of such philosophy) 'it gets them anywhere'.

I shall argue that this dilemma is unreal, on the grounds that a certain kind of non-ideological philosophy – 'conceptual analysis', if we must give it a name – can (contrary to appearances) satisfy our demands: provided only that it is properly understood and properly taught. That is a big proviso, and most of this book will be concerned with explicating it. But before entering upon this argument and explication, there is a certain amount of ground to be cleared and some initial objections to be met (or misunderstandings to be set right). For my general thesis is not a fashionable one. It is widely believed that 'conceptual analysis' or 'linguistic analysis' was a philosophical fashion current at Oxford and elsewhere some thirty or forty years ago, now largely overtaken by less rigid and less doctrinaire ways of doing philosophy: it bequeathed to us some useful lessons about the importance of linguistic clarity, but was based on some false assumptions and fatal blind spots. Even some very able philosophers seem to believe this (see Williams in Magee, 1978). It might, moreover, be objected that my distinction, between ideological 'philosophies of life' and the non-ideological philosophy of which conceptual analysis is one kind, is untenable: that (as seems to be commonly believed nowadays) all thinking is really ideological – whatever that means: and that conceptual analysis is merely one 'school' amongst many, with no particular claim to precedence. Or again, it might be thought that there could be no experts, philosophical or other, who could meet the demands mentioned earlier: in particular, that each man must choose for himself how to live and what he thinks right rather than handing such matters over to philosophers of any kind.

I do not want to confront these or other such criticisms head-on. For any such confrontation would suggest that I was defending either (a) a particular (historical) school of philosophy that flourished at a certain time and held certain doctrines, or at least (b) a particular set of doctrines, whether or not those of a particular (historical) school. I am not concerned with (a) at all: that is essentially a historical enquiry. With (b) I am only concerned in the widest possible sense of 'doctrines', if indeed there is such a sense: in other words, I do indeed believe certain procedures to be necessary or desirable in philosophy, but I take my belief to be such that, if anyone called it a 'doctrine', I should suspect that he had misunderstood it. Not all beliefs are doctrines, any more than all preferences are ideological.

That point is not as pedantic as it may seem; for there are in fact very different kinds of beliefs, principles, points of method or (to speak very generally) moves that can be made here, and the differences are very important. Characteristically, I suppose, what happens is that people adopt or reject some specific set of beliefs which it might be fair to call 'doctrines': they accept or deny the beliefs of Marxism, or Christianity, or Islam, or whatever; or else they never do anything definite enough to be described as 'accepting' or 'rejecting' – they just drift, living (as we all must) according to some set of conscious or unconscious principles, but not being concerned to question these very sharply. Nor need these beliefs be enshrined in some kind of large-scale faith or -ism; they might be very mixed, and too unstructured or low-temperature to be described as ideological. But all these are beliefs which bear *directly* on what the world is like and how we ought to live: they tell us directly what is the case and issue imperatives about what we ought to do.

By 'directly' I intend some kind of contrast with principles whose purpose may be seen as *negotiating* between, or trying to *adjudicate*, these beliefs. The contrast is like that between the advancement of particular political views – views which directly state what is or ought to be the case – and the rules of debate or procedure which govern such matters as who is

allowed to speak and for how long, how issues are to be settled
(by voting or force), and so on. The fact that these principles
bear only indirectly upon what is said does not make them less
important: indeed it is fairly clear, in this particular example,
that civilised life rests more upon the indirect principles of
procedure – upon agreements about the negotiation or adjudi-
cation of beliefs – than upon the direct force of any particular
ground-level beliefs.

There are many kinds of indirect principles or points of
procedure, even if we include only those relevant to philosophy. Quite a lot of them have to do with what might be called
the social and psychological aspects of philosophy: they concern the importance of debate and dialectic, of welcoming
criticism, of adopting a certain kind of psychological stance or
attitude, of using a certain kind of social context, and so forth.
These are commonly overlooked; and we shall be returning to
them in the last two chapters of this book. For the present, I
invite the reader to consider some indirect principles which are
more specifically to do with the *content* of what philosophers
and ideologists say. These principles are, I think, extremely
simple and obvious, not in themselves at all intellectually
complicated; nevertheless my experience is that there is immense resistance to them, and that desperate attempts are
made to avoid them, or misconstrue them, or defuse them – for
psychological reasons on which we shall also comment later
(Chapter 4). So it is worth our while to spend a little time on
them.

If – a big 'if' – a person wants to think and act reasonably or
sanely in relation to all the very different and often very
strange things that philosophers and ideologists and others tell
him, what sort of principles would he follow? He would want,
surely, to *get clear* (in a general way) about what they *meant*
when they said these things: to *make sense* of their remarks.
This would not be only, perhaps not even primarily, a matter
of looking very hard at particular words or sentences: it would
be a matter of trying to determine, still in a fairly general way,
what sort of talk they were talking, what sort of business they
were in, what sort of game they were playing. And he would
note important differences here. Just as the rules governing the
practices and writings of scientists differ from those of historians, and differ again from those of art critics or moralists,

so he would find that a great many different things went on under the heading of 'philosophy'. He would need to sort out these differences.

Let us suppose, to sharpen up the point, that he is concerned with the teaching and learning of philosophy: as a teacher, he needs to know what sort of thing to do; or as a student, what sort of thing he is in for. It might seem unnecessary to say that if we set out to teach X we must first be clear about just what X is. In practice, however, the force of such an obvious point is largely neglected: and not only in philosophy. Does 'French' mean the ability to converse in French (and about what topics?), or an appreciation of French grammar and the works of sophisticated French literature? Does 'mathematics' mean the ability to do mental arithmetic and count one's change, or a grasp of set theory and other basic logical principles? Does 'classics' mean knowledge of the Greek and Latin languages, or some familiarity with the classical world and an occasional trip to the British Museum or a Roman villa?

Rather than try to answer these questions (admittedly difficult, and involving more or less wise judgements of value or emphasis), educators tend to assume, or at least not enthusiastically to deny, that there is some kind of consensus about the nature of these subjects – about what ground a subject-title X is to cover – and then spend a great deal of time in disputing about the method, strategy, techniques, processes and (perhaps) hardware which may help us teach X more effectively. That is a very well-known way of going about things, involving a familiar ends–means model: we take the ends for granted and hurry on to the technology, where we feel more at home. But it is, surely, entirely clear that – at least broadly speaking – the methods will inevitably be a function of the sense given to X. If 'classics' is construed in one way, certain methods necessarily commend themselves: if in another, certain other and very different methods. And so, unsurprisingly, with philosophy. For nothing is gained by remarks about method which, though sound, are in effect vacuous. To take a recent example from a journal called *Teaching Philosophy* (vol. 3, no. 2, Fall 1979), not much is gained by the following injunctions:

1. Be clear about what you are setting out to do.
2. Think about, read about, and if possible discuss with

       other people what considerations are relevant to your
       topic.
  3. Gather your arguments and arrange them in a logical
       framework which is made clear in your essay.
  4. Set your material down on paper in a precise, grammati-
       cal and preferably elegant form.

Nobody of course would want to object to these: the trouble is
that they have nothing specifically to do with *philosophy*: they
would, I think, apply to more or less any essay that involved
rational and coherent thought.

    How would one try to categorise the different kinds of things
which seem to be going on under the heading 'philosophy'?
What kinds of differences would we be concerned with? Of
course we can classify various kinds of philosophy as we like,
and different categorisations suit different purposes (an ency-
clopaedist might categorise them according to which letter of
the alphabet they began with, a university administrator according to which were the cheapest to teach, a lazy student by
which had the easiest courses to pass, and so on). But it is very
difficult to avoid the question of what counts as performing *well*
in *this* (rather than that) type of enterprise; if one is (even
potentially) interested in any enterprise, one needs an idea of
what the rules of it are, what goods it is supposed to produce,
what sort of virtues and other equipment one needs for doing it
well.

    With theoretical enterprises – that is, roughly, enterprises
which are supposed to bring us some kind of knowledge – this
sort of categorisation is really an attempt to distinguish different sorts of truth: and again, we shall mean here *logically*
different sorts. 'Logically different' will mean, again briefly and
roughly, 'different in terms of the rules or methods by which
the truth emerges': for instance, the differences in terms of
evidence or tests or intellectual procedures. Thus if we say (as
many have been tempted to) that philosophy is concerned with
very general or wide questions, we shall note that questions
like "What is the universe made of?", where the answer will
have something to do with atoms or particles or waves, is very
general or wide: but we rightly classify it as scientific rather
than philosophical, because the whole methodology and all the
procedures for answering it are scientific.

The natural move to make, then, seems to be some kind of classification in terms of *types of truth*; and this has led many philosophers to make an important distinction between (1) matters of fact and (2) matters of logic. We shall discuss this in more detail later (Chapter 1), but the general idea behind the distinction is clear. It is one sort of thing to say that bachelors are useful for dinner parties, or that puppies are a nuisance around the house: another to say that bachelors are unmarried, or that puppies are young dogs. It might also be suggested that philosophers, or one kind of philosophers, are particularly concerned with (2) matters of logic: that is what distinguishes them from scientists and historians and others who are concerned with (various kinds of) fact. Such a suggestion might at least give us something which could reasonably be called 'philosophy', which was uniquely philosophical, and which dealt with a particular kind of truth – that is, logical or conceptual truth.

All that is both exceedingly sketchy and perhaps (so far as it goes) exceedingly obvious; but it does, in fact, tend to promote certain typical reactions which are worth spending a bit of time on, since they encapsulate, I believe, the main worries that prevail. I submitted these points to a large number of professional philosophers in the UK and North America, asking for comments: in general (I will not weary the reader with statistics), if we leave aside the favourable comments and other forms of agreement, the worries can be reduced to three. The first can be represented by the remark: "Why should the categories chosen for clarification reflect senses of 'philosophy' in current use, why take the latter as a starting-point?" The interest lies in the implication that one could reasonably choose categories which do *not* 'reflect senses in current use', that one could take some *other* 'starting-point'. Very well: suppose one was writing about different interpretations of (say) 'French' or different kinds of French-teaching, and started to make some categories of the various things that seemed to go on under this heading – for instance, (1) grammar and syntax of the French language, (2) appreciation of French literature, (3) history of French culture, (4) geography of France, and so forth. Now suppose somebody came along and criticised this, saying "Why choose categories reflecting senses in common use, why start with these?" We should say "How else could we start, for heaven's sake?" We're not writing about just *any* categories or interpretations of *anything*, but about different interpretations of *French* – and that limits us, at least as a starting-point, to what goes on *under that heading*. Suppose we started our categories as follows: (1) learning the twice times table, (2) learning to multiply, etc., wouldn't you say "Hey, I thought you were trying to make some helpful categories for the teaching of *French*, not mathematics!"? And if we replied "Tut, tut, we're not going to be tied down in such a servile way to 'current use' ", would you not think we were, at least, rather hard to communicate with? Indeed unless we both at least start with meaning more or less the same thing by the same words how are we to communicate at all? If we are looking at things relevant to the teaching of *philosophy*, we are similarly limited. Of course we *could* – there is no law against it – list categories that had nothing to do with the current use of the term 'philosophy'. But then for instance, the title of the journal *Teaching Philosophy* would be, to say the least, misleading (and in many parts of the world selling that title when the contents had nothing to do with what we normally meant by 'philosophy' *would* be illegal, a case of obtaining money under false pretences).

A second reaction was: "I don't see why what is *uniquely* philosophical . . . should bear on the *merits* of teaching any category." This also has some interest, because it is entirely clear that under normal conditions and in cases other than philosophy everybody does see this quite easily. If we are trying to decide whether to allot precious time in the curriculum to (say) French, or Latin, or Chinese, the debate could not be conducted intelligently (or even, I think, intelligibly) without some reference to what was *peculiar* to this or that language – that Latin uniquely trained the mind, that Chinese would be particularly useful, and so on. Again, how could one make decisions about the merits or methods of mathematical teaching without having *some* adequate idea about the peculiar nature of mathematical proof and mathematical understanding (otherwise, why consider the teaching of *mathematics* rather than of something else)? Of course uniqueness does not *prove* merit but it is *relevant*. Without clarifying what is peculiar, unique or *sui generis* we cannot even lay out the options for inspection and judgement.

The third reaction ("I have no faith that the sharp division of philosophical and empirical truth . . . can be upheld") is interesting as an example of how quickly some quite sophisticated enquiries into the nature of analytical truth can turn into a total loss of nerve (see Quine, refuted by Grice and Strawson – references in Strawson, 1967). We all know that words have meanings – that they imply such-and-such and do not imply so-and-so: if someone says that triangles have four sides or that mammals do not suckle their young or that punishment could characteristically be pleasant, we recognise conceptual errors. We recognise also the 'division' or distinction between this sort of error and an error about other kinds of facts (not about what words mean), such as thinking that there are no triangles in a certain geometrical text-book or no mammals in Australia or no punishments in Hong Kong. Is it a 'sharp' distinction? Well, differences are just differences: certainly there does not have to be any sort of sliding-scale movement or slow creepage from the empirical to the conceptual. Whatever else may (with more or less credibility and profit) be questioned here, the existence of some kind of distinction is not in dispute amongst serious people (see later, Chapter 1).

All this also seems excessively obvious, and no doubt these and other critics would agree. The general point I want to make is this: it is *not* so much at the level of particular issues that misunderstanding flourishes, but rather at some level (perhaps only semi-conscious) of the mind where one person has some image or received doctrine of what the other person stands for and therefore must be saying. 'Linguistic phenomenology' (as Austin, 1961, p. 130, called it) has been a particularly prominent victim: to some temperaments it somehow *must* be true that Austin, or 'Oxford philosophers', or 'linguistic analysts' or somebody must hold certain 'theses' or make substantive 'assumptions' about the merits of ordinary language, or theoretical distinctions in logic like the analytic–synthetic distinction, or have some sort of substantive philosophical position held *a priori*. (In just such a way many people are called 'utilitarians', as if that meant something sufficiently clear to be helpful: as, arguably, it does not.) They must *stand for* something. But in fact the only things they 'stand for' may be procedural, not substantive: they may think we ought to be really clear about what we mean when we say what we say. If anyone were to deny the importance of that, I should not know how to talk to him; but if it is accepted seriously, it turns out to be a much longer job than might be thought, making heavy demands upon the patience of those who would prefer either to run into the arms of some ideological position or retreat into the comparative safety and seclusion of philosophical history or the explication of others' views. The *dialectic* required for getting clear is psychologically very difficult to sustain: it is quite unsurprising that the time spent on such dialectic is, in most philosophy classes, very small. Engaging (preferably face to face, but the written word can substitute) in this dialogue is crucial, because only dialectical criticism challenges our autism. Of course it is easier to run off or to get angry, like Cephalus and Thrasymachus in the *Republic*; and of course we should expect theories of philosophy according to which we can legitimately escape, nullify or dominate such dialogue – just as patients in non-directive analytic psychotherapy will find some theory to justify their own dislike of the treatment (see later, Chapter 4).

I need to emphasise here that I am trying to describe only *one* category of activity which might reasonably count as 'philosophy'. To argue that this is the best, or the only proper, or the most reputable kind of philosophy would be in two ways premature: first, because we are not yet clear (as I hope to make clear in this book) what it is and what it can do; and secondly, because we do not have an adequate taxonomy or set of categories for what might go on under the heading 'philosophy', such that we could compare this category with others. Of course we can make some rough distinctions. We can talk about: (1) formal logic – a tolerably clear category in itself, though arguably more like mathematics than like other sorts of philosophy; (2) some kind of ideological instruction, either (a) to persuade people into some ideology, or (b) simply to get them to understand it; (3) sociological or historical explanation of the effects of some ideology on various people, perhaps the same as what is commonly called 'the history of ideas' (and why should this not be classified as history or sociology rather than philosophy?); and (4) some rather nebulous activities under headings like 'critical thinking' (for instance, in Lipman's work at the Institute for the Advancement of Philosophy for Children; see Lipman, 1977) – but why should this be thought uniquely philosophical? Trying to sort all this out, however, would be a major task in itself: one well worth attempting, but not here.

It has to be said, though, that even in considering this undertaking much the same kinds of fears and accusations are liable to crop up. The very process of analysis and categorisation must represent the 'English analytic school' with its belief in 'ordinary language': and surely the analyst must have concealed some value-judgements somewhere – the whole thing must somehow be a subtle attempt to sell a particular line. Is he not really trying to propagate the bourgeois western values that have always gone along with middle-class academic contexts? – and so on and so forth. The (admittedly depressing) fact is that we are confronted here with a vicious circle: in order to show that *one* legitimate category to be included under the heading 'philosophy' is conceptual or analytic enquiry, we have to advance arguments which are themselves part of such an enquiry. We shall not get agreement about the importance of common usage and of distinguishing what is distinctive, in particular the difference between logical and empirical truth, unless people are agreed that the arguments are worth attending to – that clarity is *important*. In practice, and in some circles, I doubt whether much sincere or at least heartfelt agreement on these obvious points exists. Heels are dragged, objections made, difficulties adumbrated: palpably lacking is – what one surely has a right to expect from those interested in teaching philosophy – a passionate concern to be remorselessly clear about just what we are teaching or just what we are to mean by 'philosophy'.

Whatever else we may want to say about it, we can maintain that the category of 'conceptual analysis' may now be seen *not* (only or primarily) as the property of one particular philosophical school, but rather as at least partly equivalent to whatever processes are required for understanding each other and getting really clear about what we mean when we say things. Now it seems tolerably obvious that this category has a certain logical and temporal priority: that is to say, we ought to get clear about what we mean *before* engaging in other activities – in particular, before claiming that what is said is true or false or important, or historically influential, or believed by so-and-so, or whatever. For how can we make such judgements if we do not know what the words mean, if we are not clear about just *what* is being said? It would, I suppose, be possible for somebody (rather after the manner of certain religious people) to say "Never mind about what these words mean, just repeat them and they'll sink in, it's a matter of faith": but even that is not good enough here, since philosophy in any sense must involve some degree of *understanding* of what is said, not just verbal repetition. So our first job is to understand each other.

Having outlined this argument, how should we react if someone still said that we were trying to impose some particular value-judgement about the merits of a particular philosophical school, 'linguistic analysis', on all philosophers? The argument (we tell him) is of this rough form: if you are concerned with truth and understanding, you have to be concerned with what people mean, because there is a logical link between the two. If someone said "I wish to advance Marxist theories of such-and-such because they're true, but I don't want to be bothered with questions about what the words in them mean", we should not understand him. So (we continue) we are just holding up a logical or conceptual link, a link of meaning between 'being concerned for truth' and 'getting clear what's meant' – not very exciting, we fear, but there it is. And if he still insisted that our remarks were partisan or ideological, or indeed anything else but glaringly obvious, we should probably not want to argue with him any more.

To any such accusation of glaring obviousness or boredom I immediately plead guilty: it is, indeed, certainly very obvious, but psychologically (and, when it comes to the hard work of detail, intellectually) very demanding, procedures by which most serious philosophy stands or falls. It is the first business of any philosopher to get clear about what these procedures are, and to make his pupils clear: as Austin also said, clarity must be the first word in philosophy, if not the last. It will be time enough, to pronounce on the merits of other styles of philosophising, or senses of 'philosophy', when we have enough equipment and enough practice in getting clear.

All this is, of course, so far very rough and sketchy. We are not yet clear about what sort of thing 'conceptual analysis' or 'linguistic phenomenology' is, about how it can be well or badly done, and (above all) about just what sort of goods it can provide us with – about what it can do. Nevertheless, it is this sort of philosophy (this sense of 'philosophy') that I want to concentrate on for the rest of this book, because I believe that it relates most closely and effectively to the desire with which we began – the desire to know what is real and what is valuable.

1 Mistakes about Conceptual Analysis

I have suggested that if we want to know – putting it brutally – what use or good philosophers are, we shall best interpret the question "What is philosophy?" along the lines of "What *kind of truth*, and what kind of arguments for it, do philosophers uniquely dispense?" or "How do philosophers as against, say, historians or scientists or literary critics or psychologists distinguish themselves as truth-finders?"

If we do not accept some tradition which distinguishes 'philosophy' from the erection or sale of certain 'philosophies' or 'philosophies of life', this question seems hard to answer. Various outlooks, 'world-views', creeds, 'faiths to live by', etc. are produced, to which we may be more or less attracted; but even when it is clear that these are *supposed* to be true (rather than just appealing, or beautiful, or moving, or politically effective), it is not clear *how* they are supposed to be true: that is, what kinds of arguments or evidence they are based on. Do they rely on some kind of facts, and if so what kind? Also, if so, are not these facts already wielded by some other expert? Thus if Marxism – assuming, what is untrue, that we know just what to put under that heading – is supposed to rest on historical or economic facts, presumably it must be some kind of historical or economic theory: but then why call it *philosophy*? Do they rely on pure logic? But then it is not easy to see (a) how pure logic can produce outlooks and creeds of such a substantive and detailed kind, or (b) why these outlooks and creeds should be so diverse and often mutually contradictory.

Within such a tradition, and more particularly within the way of doing philosophy (or of conceiving philosophy) that has grown up in the UK, the Commonwealth countries, the USA and elsewhere in the last fifty years or so, the question seems more easily answerable. Philosophers are supposed to deal in what are called 'conceptual' truths. These are, if you like, truths of logic: but not or not only of formal logic or mathematics. Philosophers deal with concepts we use every day, not or not only – certainly not centrally – with technical or highly-specialised concepts (see p. 36ff.). The idea is that concepts, marked of course by certain words in natural languages, are logically related to others in various ways. Often – as with the simple examples which we usually rely on – these relations are very obvious: triangles must (logically) have three sides, bachelors must be unmarried, and so on. In a slightly less obvious way, the concept marked by (say) 'learn' may be seen to imply some idea of mastering something, and of attending to certain standards or goals: that marked by 'discipline' to imply some idea of obedience to an established authority: that marked by 'society' or 'social communication' to imply some notion of a norm of truth-telling. The philosopher's business, it is believed, is to exhibit these conceptual (or logical, or linguistic) relationships: to show what can be said with consistency and coherency and intelligibility, and what cannot.

The ultimate weapon, so to speak, of philosophy as thus described is the notion of contradiction. If someone said, for instance, "Human beings should have no rules when dealing with each other", the philosopher would try to show that this was internally incoherent or contradictory: that there was something logically contained in the idea, or concept, of human interaction (as against, say, billiard balls bumping into each other) which itself implied the existence of rules: for instance, the rules of language which are usually obeyed when people talk to each other and which alone make communication possible. The philosopher simply (!) shows what is implied by what one says, when one takes time off to think properly about it: "If you say A, then that means you have to say B as well, but that you can't coherently say C", and so on.

There is a great deal more to say about this, some of which I shall try to say shortly; but meanwhile it is enough to note that the *general* principles of this practice are fairly clear. They have been stated in various elementary introductions to philosophy, and there is an enormous amount of philosophical work which exemplifies them. I want to press on to a question about what these principles can achieve: what their force, values and limitations are. For I think (indeed I am sure) that both the general account of these principles and the practice of them in actual philosophical work leave many people dissatisfied. They feel that the very most the philosopher can do is to show that failure to philosophise – failure to attend to the conceptual implications of what one says – may lead not only to muddle and incoherence, but to great danger. For instance, if Germans around the 1930s had thought seriously and philosophically about notions marked by 'Aryan blood', 'sub-men', 'racial purity' and so on, it is possible that a lot of bloodshed would have been averted. This is not just a question of being linguistically tidy, of 'defining one's terms' in order to be intellectually respectable; it is a matter of needing to get clear in order to avert the pressures of fantasy and prejudice, which operate disastrously in the real world when we fail to inspect and check them, and which emerge in a misuse of language.

However, this is an essentially negative or therapeutic power – though none the less important for that. On this account – so far as we have taken it, at least – the philosopher cannot tell you any important truths *about the world* in a positive sort of way. All he can do (though this is plenty, and alone would justify philosophy) is to prevent you getting into a muddle and allowing your prejudices and fantasies to emerge unchecked into action. For (the story goes) the philosopher deals, as we have seen, only with conceptual (logical) truths, not with matters of fact: these he leaves to the scientist, or the historian, or to whoever it may be that deals with particular kinds of fact.

A good, and perhaps central, example of this can be found in moral or political philosophy. The story might be something like this: "Different people have different political or moral values: they talk about, and justify what they do under such terms as, 'love' or 'democracy' or 'justice' or whatever. Some people admire one sort of system, others another sort. Now the philosopher can help by making these (very different) views internally consistent. He can tell you what the concepts you use in spelling out your view imply, and what they cannot imply. If you talk of 'justice', and mean what you say, then such-and-such follows, and so-and-so cannot follow. But what the philosopher cannot do is to tell you what concepts to start with, what system to adopt in the first place. That is a matter for each individual to settle for himself: philosophers are – nowadays at least – not out to proselytise or convert or preach. Once you have got some game going, he can perhaps clarify the rules for you: but he cannot tell you what games to play."

Something like this is perhaps still the prevailing orthodoxy today. In particular, stress is laid on the fact that philosophers do not take sides when it comes to 'substantive' issues, whether of a moral/political nature or not. They do not tell you how the world is: that is for natural and social scientists. They do not tell you how it ought to be: that each man must judge for himself. There is still a very considerable fear of philosophers seeming to be 'experts' in the old-time sense of sages who have some kind of magic insight, denied to the rest of us, in virtue of which they ought to be obeyed. Part of the reason for this fear may simply be that the prevailing fashion is very much against the idea of 'experts', at least of this kind. It seems undemocratic and anti-egalitarian. Moreover, the kind of people who are attracted to philosophy – in liberal countries where this kind of philosophy is practised – are perhaps more than usually keen on intellectual autonomy: they are good or even paradigmatic liberals, against censorship, in favour of open politics, against anything that smacks of totalitarianism or indoctrination, in favour of self-determination and the other liberal virtues. There is, however, still something very fishy about this position.

What is fishy is this. One of two things: either we believe that it is, in a fairly strict sense, *arbitrary* what concepts we choose to base our lives on and what moral and political values we assert – in the sense that no good reasons can be given for one or the other set of concepts or values; or we believe, though we may be unclear about how to prove, that things are not arbitrary in this sense – that there *are reasons* for jumping this way or that. I doubt whether anyone seriously believes the former; but if he did, it would be hard to see much value in philosophy. For what would be the *point* of clearing up muddles, exhibiting conceptual implications, producing clarity and consistency, and (in general) philosophising, if we did not think that this would help us to choose more *correctly*? Why bother to make the Nazis think about what they say and claim to believe, if this will not put them in a *better* frame of mind than before? On the other hand, if there actually are criteria by which we should make our moral and political judgements – if we can use good or bad reasons in this department of life – then it ought to be the philosopher's business to tell us what they are: and this surely brings in the idea of *some* kind of expertise. The expertise would be that of a person who, whilst not issuing particular orders, nevertheless showed us in a general sort of way what *sort* of orders we should attend to: who gave us a proper understanding of the methodology, as it were, of doing morality or politics or science or history or whatever. And that would be a very important sort of expert indeed.

I believe the latter to be true. To give a brief preview of the reasons why I believe it to be true – and the point is independent of the particular examples of morality and politics – it seems *not* to be entirely a matter of individual human choice to determine what concepts we shall start with. As human beings, we are *landed with* a great many concepts which we *have* to use: 'have to', not because of any empirical compulsion, but because these concepts are a logically inevitable part of the furniture of any conceivable world. I need not give many examples here; but it seems clear, for instance, that basic categories like time, cause and effect, space itself, choice, the notions of 'good' and 'bad', and the various emotions that are generated by these preconditions, certain implications which must be true of *any* human society (like the norm of truth-telling), and a good many other things are – so to speak – *given*. They are the limits or the necessary furniture not only of our world but of any possible world with people in it. And if that is so, it is obviously of great practical importance that everyone should realise it.

Before going into more detail, however, we need to look a bit more closely at two ways in which (as I see it) philosophers have denied their own powers, or at least seemed to do so. We need to see our way through (and out of) two doctrines that are and have for some years been widely publicised, which seem at first sight almost as if they had been specifically designed to reject the ordinary man's desire for help. Briefly, the general public has received the impression – I say 'the impression', because I want to leave it open whether philosophers in general actually held or hold anything like these doctrines – that (1) philosophers cannot tell us what the world is like but can tell us only about concepts or meanings, that conclusions of 'fact', or 'substance', cannot be derived from 'purely formal' or 'conceptual' considerations, and (2) neither philosophers nor (it might appear) anyone else can tell us how to live, because 'values' can be derived neither from purely conceptual considerations, nor from 'facts'.

Naturally the brief words in which I have set out these doctrines are not at all clear: nor is it clear whether they should really be called 'doctrines' at all (they might be seen as summaries induced, perhaps wrongly, from the general trend of some fairly recent philosophical work): nor whether any philosopher would really wish to stand by them (in this brief form, almost certainly not: though when forced into brevity many philosophers say something remarkably like them – see below). Nevertheless, I suspect that many people – including some philosophers – have not only taken these doctrines as somehow essentially part of, or connected with, the whole enterprise of conceptual analysis, but have as a result turned away from that enterprise and (perhaps) taken up something else instead: some kind of historical or sociological study of concepts or ideas, or some kind of ideology.

(A)   FACTS AND CONCEPTUAL TRUTH

There are, I think, two basic points – no doubt obvious in themselves and perhaps not seriously disputed by any philosopher – which largely defuse any force there may be in the former thesis:

(1) The first can perhaps most readily be grasped by asking whether or not it is a fact that (say) mammals suckle their young, or that circles enclose more area for less perimeter than any other figure. If uncontaminated by philosophical theses and willing to speak ordinary English, we should have no hesitation in saying that these were facts, and that by being told them we had been told something true about mammals and about circles (*not* about the words 'mammal' and 'circle' or the concepts they mark). Nor should we hesitate to say that a person might be given useful informa-

tion in this way: he wants, perhaps, an animal to demonstrate breast-feeding to his children, and we tell him "Buy a mammal"; to enclose as much land by as short a circuit as possible, and we tell him "Drive your plough in a circle". If 'empirical' means anything sufficiently clear to be worth using here, we might say that they were empirical facts: facts, certainly, 'about the world' and about our experiences of the world. Mammals *do* suckle their young; circles *are* the most economical figures. Indeed somebody might notice these facts, and come to regard them as well-substantiated generalisations, without tangling with the notion of conceptual truth or meaning at all.

Now if some philosopher tells us that it is not a matter of fact that mammals suckle their young, how shall we understand him? He will say perhaps "Of course it is *true* that mammals suckle their young, but that is because we mean by 'mammals' 'creatures that suckle their young'. The only fact here is a linguistic fact – the fact that 'mammals' means 'creatures that suckle their young'. "And he may go on to say "It *must* be the case that mammals suckle their young", or "We wouldn't call them 'mammals' if they didn't" and go on to talk about analytic or logical or conceptual truths as against truths of fact or experience. But now this makes what he says even more mysterious: if it is inconceivable, or contradictory, or in some way logically out of the question that mammals should not suckle their young, that seems to add even more force to the fact that they do, not to remove the fact. The philosopher has given us reasons for believing that mammals suckle their young which endorse or transform any weaker reasons we might have had: as he says, "It *must* be the case."

What the philosopher really needs to say is, not that this is not a fact, nor even that it is a different kind of fact, but simply that the reasons which make it a fact – which make the proposition true – are different: that the way in which we would naturally argue for the proposition, the kind of enquiries we undertake in order to investigate the truth, the grounds on which it rests, are all unlike those which we use in asserting that, for instance, mammals evolved at a later stage than reptiles, or that mammals tend to be more intelligent than other sorts of animals. For these latter facts

would normally be defended by observation and experience of the visible world, not by any appeal to language
and concepts. The temptation to describe them as a different kind of fact arises here; but it has to be resisted. It is a
fact *in the world* that a mammal will suckle its young; it is a
fact of *language* that 'mammal' means 'suckling its young';
and we can arrive at the former fact by means of the latter.
"If something is a mammal, then it will suckle its young" is
a fact of just the same kind, though not backed by the same
kind of reasons, as "If something is a mammal, then it is
likely to be more intelligent than a member of another
species". In answer to the question "Will this mammal
suckle its young?" it would be elliptic to reply simply
"'Mammal' means 'suckling its young'": the more natural reply is "*Yes, because* 'mammal' means "suckling its
young' ".

This point does not have to follow from, or lead to, any
idea about there being necessary truths, or essences, or
inexpellable features of human life, which are not dependent on analytic or conceptual truth. It is this which has led
some philosophers (see, e.g., Quinton, 1973, pp. 270ff.) to
describe these necessary features as 'conventional' rather
than as matters of fact. But this description implies (a) 'that
the conventions actually in force could have been different
from what they are' (p. 273), and (b) that what the conventions give us can only be a logical entailment or identity.
Both (a) and (b) are, in a way, quite true: but they are also
misleading. If (a) means just that linguistic or notational
conventions could have been different – that 'mammal', for
instance, might be used to mean 'reptile' – that is true: but
there are certain features of any form of human life which
will always, so long as there are men who speak language,
require conventions that are essentially similar in force if
not in form: for instance, so long as there are men, there
will be *some* convention – not necessarily using the actual
words 'man' and 'body' – which connects men with embodiment. If we say for instance, that "to speak a language is
still a choice and the law of contradiction still a convention" (ibid.), the implication is that there could be men to
whom these features would not apply: and that seems
incoherent. Similarly if (b) means that there is, as it were,

'nothing in' an analytic truth like "Mammals suckle their
young" except the relationship of conceptual implication or
identity of meaning between the two terms 'mammal' and
'suckling its young', that is true: but if it means that a
person cannot in the real world get new information about
the real world by means of this relationship, that is false –
and this is what leads us to say that by understanding the
relationship we come to appreciate a *fact*. We may say, if
we like, that the information is only new to him (if he
understood the concepts he would have it already), but that
does not seem to be a decisive objection: the same goes for
facts reached by new empirical information – if one had it
already, it would not be new.

I offer another example of a somewhat different kind:

> Even in geometry, where the enterprise [sc. of deriving
> facts from conceptual arguments] is most inviting, they
> will hold that enquiry into the concept *circle* (into the
> meaning of the word 'circle') can yield only analytic
> truths; it cannot show us anything about what can or
> cannot take place in the world. If anybody says, for
> example, that we can prove by conceptual enquiry that
> there cannot be, in the physical world, a circle whose
> radii are not equal, we shall reply that all he has proved
> is that, if there is a figure in the physical world whose
> radii are not equal, we cannot *call* it a circle – that is, he
> has proved something, not about the world, but about
> language.   (Hare, 1970)

But (1) if we cannot "prove by conceptual enquiry that
there cannot be, in the physical world, a circle whose radii
are not equal", how *are* we supposed to prove it? (2) The
man proves, not that "if there is a figure in the physical
world whose radii are not equal, we cannot *call* it a circle",
but that such a figure cannot *be* a circle. (People can and
commonly do *call* things what they like: if we try to compromise and say that he has proved that we cannot *properly*
call it a circle, that will be because it *isn't* one.) (3) Ge-
ometers commonly argue roughly as follows: "By 'circle'
we will mean a figure the perimeter of which is at all points
equidistant from its centre: so if you draw a line from the

centre (C) to any two points on the perimeter (A and B), CA must equal CB. Further, if you draw the diameter (XY) and construct a triangle from its ends to any point (Z) on the perimeter, the angle XZY will be a right angle, because . . ." and so on. These are not empirical arguments, but conceptual or deductive ones. Now what can be meant by saying that what they prove is 'about language'? The arguments are about *circles*, or the properties of circles: and in so far as we want to say (as we usually do) that there are circles in 'the world', the arguments are 'about the world'.

Actually the 'enterprise' is not 'most inviting' in the case of geometry or mathematics generally; for we can claim that in a strict sense, or a sense in which mathematical proofs apply, circles and the like are not in 'the world' at all (lines have no thickness, points no magnitude, and so on). For a different reason, examples which make use of tautologies or near-tautologies are also uninviting: if we say that a puppy is a young dog, or that bachelors are unmarried, it is at least as plausible (in many speech-acts) to comment that we are giving information about the words 'puppy' or 'bachelor' (rather than about the things) as to claim the opposite. The truth is that what we are trying to do and what we succeed in doing will depend at least partly on our intentions and on the context. Suppose a boy is told that he is getting a puppy for Christmas: he has not heard the word, but he knows what a young dog is: we say to him "A puppy is a young dog". We may be, albeit indirectly and *by means of* a linguistic truth or piece of translation, informing him about what sort of thing he is going to get for Christmas: he buys a kennel, lays in a store of dog-food, etc. If that is not informing him about the world, what is? (Compare telling someone in a classroom that 'pericolo' is the Italian for 'danger' and telling him the same thing when he is driving his car very fast and sees a notice with 'pericolo' on it.)

Part of the trouble here comes with one obvious difficulty which philosophers have run into when trying to distinguish analytic from synthetic propositions: that we cannot combine brevity with clarity if we oppose 'language' to 'the world', or 'the meanings of words' to 'the facts' or 'experience', for – obviously enough – language is in or part of the world, and what words mean is a matter of fact or experience. For if I say " 'Chien' in French means what 'dog' means in English", that proposition is clearly about 'language' or 'the meanings of words'; yet, just as clearly, no one wants to say that it does not convey a fact 'about the world' or 'in experience'. The point holds, even if we make the distinction not in terms of what the proposition is supposed to be about, but in terms of how it is supposed to be verified: verifying whether 'chien' is equivalent to 'dog' is, after all, much like verifying any other empirical fact – verifying what the equivalent to £2.41 is in American dollars, for instance. This shows well enough, indeed, that the criterion of being 'about language', commonly supposed to be a reinforcement to or aspect of the criterion of 'depending for its validity on the meanings of words', is actually inconsistent with it. Propositions that are (one might say) overtly about language – such as (1) " 'Mammal' means 'suckling one's young' ", have no smack of logical necessity about them, just because they make overt and empirically falsifiable claims about words. On the other hand, propositions which are not overtly – or, I think, at all – 'about language', such as (2) "Mammals suckle their young", can be seen as analytic or logically necessary, because we can take certain verbal rules as given (not as offered for inspection). To put this another way: the verification for (1) 'depends on the meanings of words' where those meanings are *not*, when we try to verify it, taken as settled or given; (2) also 'depends on the meanings of words', but in a different sense of 'depends' – its truth comes or flows from (hangs on) the meanings of words, but it does not turn on them (as if they were in doubt).

Some philosophers, as we noted earlier (p. 9) have spoken as if they did not believe in analytic truth (thus defined): but that can only be because they take it to be something other than it is. For the existence of analytic truth follows from the existence of words. Roughly, words must have meaning if they are to be words, and the meaning must remain sufficiently constant for us to use the words effectively: words may change their meaning (though this is a rarer and a slower process than is often supposed), but they must remain intelligible and therefore, for however short a time, consistent in what they denote. At any one time, then, any word must entail or imply some things and disallow or rule out others. Today the word 'yes' implies (roughly) 'I agree' or 'By all means' or 'Certainly', and the word 'no' implies 'Not at all', 'By no means', 'Certainly not', or 'I don't agree'. So today some such remark as "People who say 'yes' agree", is analytically true. If tomorrow we reverse the meanings of 'yes' and 'no', then tomorrow it would be analytically false.

(2) More usually, and more cautiously, philosophers say that facts 'about the world', or empirical facts, or whatever we want to call them, cannot be established by conceptual argument *alone*. The idea is, I suppose, that there has to be some kind of empirical or experiental input if there is to be a similar output. To use our previous example, we might set out a syllogism as follows:

1. There are some mammals in that part of the zoo:
2. 'Mammals' means 'animals which suckle their young':
3. Some animals in that part of the zoo suckle their young.

Without the empirical input of 1., and left only with the linguistic truth of 2., we should not be able to arrive at 3.: we should not know anything about what was going on in the zoo or anywhere in the world, but only about the meaning of a word.

That is perfectly true, but it seems wrong to describe the situation by saying that facts 'cannot be established by conceptual argument alone', partly because such a phrase carries the implication that some *other* kind of *argument* is always needed to establish them: and that, in the example above, seems not to be true. In that example, no new facts are added from the pool of sense-experience or scientific observation, no empirical generalisations adduced, and no argument other than a conceptual one used. We start, indeed, with an empirical fact in 1.; but by the time we have taken in 3. nothing has happened except conceptual enlightenment, yet we possess what any English-speaker would call (if uncorrupted by philosophical theory) a new fact. In the same way, it may be an empirical fact that John is bigger than Mary, who is bigger than Jim: will anyone now say either that it is not an empirical fact that John is bigger than Jim, or that we have reached this conclusion by something other than conceptual argument?

What we should say is, not that some other kind of *argument* is needed (or, still worse, that only empirical arguments can generate empirical facts), but that conceptual arguments have to *relate* to things in the world if they are to tell us more about things in the world. "If A is bigger than B, and B bigger than C, then A is bigger than C" is a logical schema and as such tells us nothing about anything in the world: there must be empirical input, we must know that A and B and C are represented in the world by John and Mary and Jim, that the concepts have *application*. But this is hardly a very frightening or a very severe demand: one would expect most of the concepts which philosophers – certainly linguistic philosophers – are interested in to have application: that is, some chance of extra-linguistic reference. One would expect some cases at least in which there would actually *be* mammals and circles and people of different sizes to talk about. Indeed it is rather hard to think of cases where this would not be so. "Unicorns have horns" is not very informative about physically-existing animals, but informative about animals in story-books or heraldry: and even though the deductive arguments of pure mathematics relate to ideally-defined circles, lines and so on, nevertheless circles and lines in the physical world are sufficiently like the ideal for mathematics to be informatively applied. The (fairly obvious) reason for this is that language and concepts are unlikely to be merely idle: we have them because we want to *do* something with them, to apply them. We might try to imagine a genuinely artificial language which no one ever spoke or used except for philosophical purposes, by the rules of which, say, 'sqump' implied 'squizzle', and where we would feel quite safe in saying that this conceptual truth could never yield factual information, since 'sqump' and 'squizzle' had (*ex hypothesi*) no reference to human experience whatsoever. Actually, it is not even clear that this should be called a *language*: one might call it a kind of game – but in any case this is not how language normally works.

Facts about mammals and circles may not strike us as terribly interesting: I have been anxious only to establish the point that philosophers can tell us facts – that there is nothing peculiar in saying that conceptual arguments can show us facts, and a great deal peculiar in saying that they cannot. Just what facts the philosopher can tell us and how important they may be – in particular, whether they would satisfy the desires with which we began (that is, for the philosopher to give us wide and deep understanding about reality, to tell us important and permanent truths about the world) – we shall consider later.

(B)   VALUES AND EXPERTISE

The second thesis or doctrine is a good deal vaguer, and any brief statement of it must sound like a parody. Perhaps it will be best to quote from a dialogue with one well-known philosopher who appears to represent the doctrine:

Magee   When you said . . . that the good moral philosopher wouldn't tell us what to do, you said something exceedingly important to our present discussion. A lot of people come to philosophy wanting to be told how to live – or wanting to be given an explanation of the world, and with it an explanation of life – but it seems to me that to have at least the former desire is to want to abnegate personal responsibility. One shouldn't *want* to be told how to live. And therefore one shouldn't come to philosophy looking for definitive answers. It's an entirely different thing to seek *clarification* of one's life, or clarification of the issues involved in particular problems which confront one, so that one can more effectively take responsibility for oneself and make decisions with a fuller, clearer understanding of what is at stake.

Berlin   It is a painful thing that you are saying – but unlike
           most moralists, I agree with it. Most people do
           want to be given answers.

Later Berlin adds:

It is not the business of the moral philosopher,
any more than it is the business of the novelist, to
guide people in their lives. His business is to face
them with the issues, with the range of possible
courses of action, to explain to them what they
could be choosing and why. He should endeavour
to illuminate the factors involved, to reveal the
fullest range of possibilities and their implications,
to show the character of each possibility, not in
isolation but as an element in a wider context,
perhaps of an entire form of life. He should show,
moreover, how the opening of one door may lead
to the opening or shutting of other doors – in other
words, to reveal the unavoidable incompatibility
of, the clash between, some values – often incom-
mensurable values, or, to put it in a slightly different way, point to the loss and gain involved in an
action, an entire way of life, often not in quanti-
tative terms, but in terms of absolute principles or
values, which cannot always be harmonized.
When a moral philosopher has in this fashion
placed a course of action in its moral context,
identified its position on a moral map, related its
character, motive, goal to the constellation of
values to which it belongs, drawn out its probable
consequences and its relevant implications, provided arguments for it or against it, or both for
and against it, with all the knowledge, understanding, logical skill and moral sensibility that he
possesses – then he has done his job as a philosophical adviser. It is not his business to preach or
exhort or praise or condemn, only to illuminate: in
this way he can help, but it is then for each
individual or group, in the light (of which there
can never be enough) of what they believe and

seek after, to decide for themselves. The philosopher can do no more than make as clear as he can what is at stake. But that is to do a very great deal. (Magee, 1978, pp. 32–3)

It will not, I hope, seem merely polemical (and unfairly polemical at that, since the text is of a broadcast dialogue, not of an article in a philosophical journal) to offer some criticisms of what is said here: for it is, in fact, a very good example of its kind – good, that is, as representing very clearly a somewhat *general* trend of thought or feeling, perhaps still the most common in liberal societies amongst philosophers (and certainly amongst non-philosophers). The difficulty is to decide just what such people want to say. For instance, Magee says "One shouldn't *want* to be told how to live": but if (of course only if) there are better or worse ways of living for some person, why should he not want to be told what they are? Does he really mean "One shouldn't want to be *told* how to live", with 'told' meaning something like 'just given the answers without the reasons', or even 'commanded'? And is it really 'an entirely different thing to seek clarification'? Suppose someone makes it clear to me that my life is a mess, or that I would be much better off living in this way rather than that? Berlin says "It is not the business of the moral philosopher, any more than it is the business of the novelist, to guide people in their lives" – and then goes on to describe a process which precisely is a process of guidance, and is carried out by someone Berlin subsequently describes, quite correctly, as an 'adviser'. Similarly if the philosopher is to 'point to the loss and gain involved in an action', and has 'provided arguments for it', then clearly he does to that extent 'praise or condemn'. Again, if he 'is to assess the reasons for and against', is he not thereby likely – sometimes, at least – to indicate which is right?

Several different ideas, in themselves more or less respectable in point of intelligibility if not in point of truth, may lie behind this kind of talk. (1) There is first the conceptual thesis that (cutting a long story far too short) judgements of value, or about how to live, are actually outside the scope of reason, that there are no 'right answers' (either for men in general or differing from one individual to another), that there is no 'objective' truth here that the philosopher or anyone else could guide people towards. (2) There is the conceptual thesis that there are certain limitations on *how* a person can arrive at a view (right or wrong, wise or unwise) about 'values' or 'how to live', that in various important senses he has to do this for himself or under his own steam or without compulsion, that he cannot be *forced* or simply *told* to value such-and-such. (3) There is the substantive moral or political or perhaps even metaphysical thesis that he *ought* not to be forced or told: it robs people of personality and dignity to answer for them, whether they give the right or wrong answer. (4) There is a methodological view, or perhaps several views, about the limitations on the powers of *philosophy* to tell people how to live: the philosopher can 'illuminate' in various ways, but not 'tell us the answers'. All these merit discussion in their own right: but for the present we can cut through them by asking the kind of questions which the layman might ask the philosopher: "Are there more or less reasonable ways of making up one's mind about what to do and how to live? You may not be able to tell me the answers: but can you tell me how to get the answers? Are there, as it were, certain principles of reason or procedures or pieces of mental equipment that I need to attend to rather than certain other principles or procedures or pieces? Or can I just go about my enquiry in any way I like? Is there such a thing as being 'good at' this enquiry, and if so what does it consist of? How do I conduct the enquiry *well*?"

It seems to me that philosophers can respond positively to this, as indeed some do (see, e.g., Hare in Magee, 1978, and elsewhere). But much resistance to the idea often derives mistakenly from particular theories about 'ethics' or 'the language of morals', according to which – to put it roughly – 'assertions of value' are not amenable to the same kind of proof as that to which 'factual assertions' are amenable, or perhaps not amenable to proof at all. Whatever the truth (or sense) of these theories, they are not decisively relevant to the question of expertise. Assertions about the qualities or value of works of art are plainly in some ways more nebulous, or at least different, when contrasted with historical or scientific assertions: yet most of us feel no hesitation in saying that there are literary or artistic critics who are in some sense more expert than the rest of us. We can say this without either (a) being able to give a clear account of the logic of what they assert (of 'aesthetics'), or (b) being able to specify by any exact criteria who these experts are. And this is because we are, at least, quite clear that there is such a thing as 'being good at' interpreting and judging works of art – however many footnotes, so to speak, we may want to add to this.

If there were not, in some sense, such a thing as 'being good at answering moral questions', moral matters would be 'arbitrary' in the strongest possible sense: that is, there would be no methodology, procedural principles, points to be attended to, relevant experiences to be gained, etc. which could be recommended to anybody. Nobody in fact believes this: we all know quite well (and many philosophers say so at length) that people should attend to language, think straight, understand their fellow men, and so forth. All that is required for the notion of 'moral expertise' is that *some* elements of procedure, or *some* attributes of the moralist, should be able to be seen as desirable – for instance, that he should be aware of his own emotions, or understand the principle of universalisability, or whatever we may think. If we did not believe something like this, we should be content to settle moral issues by chance (throwing dice): and notions marked by such terms as 'wisdom', 'insight', 'understanding', etc. would, in this context, make no sense to us.

Part of the trouble here may be a simple failure to distinguish between (1) formal procedures of 'proof' in the area of morality and other areas, and (2) the attributes or techniques of the *person* who attempts to solve his moral problems. The ambiguity inheres in such remarks as "There are no agreed standards for determining whether a soul or a city is healthy or diseased, just or unjust . . ." (Bambrough, 1967, pp. 102–3). This is true if it means that we do not all accept the same 'ultimate ideals', 'first principles', 'ends', etc.: false if it means that we do not all accept the relevance of certain *attributes* in *people* for determining whether . . .'. It would be surprising if any sane man, for instance, did not accept that moralists should be wise, careful, experienced, insightful, and so on: so in an important sense there *are* 'agreed standards for determining'. Some of these standards, though not all, would be similar to those we demand of 'expert critics' in aesthetic matters.

But the main trouble, I suspect, arises from a dislike of the idea that someone else (the 'expert') can 'do my morality for me', so to speak. In some parts of morality this is logically impossible: *not* because one man's opinion is as good as another's, but because in these areas morality does not consist of having an opinion at all. Thus nobody can love my wife for me, or stop smoking for me – just as no critic can appreciate Shakespeare or Rubens for me. (How much of this area would survive technological aids – e.g. some sort of mechanical nagging device in my head to keep me up to the mark of my moral decisions – is an interesting question: but the part concerned with feelings and attitudes would certainly survive.) But in the area of determining 'the right thing to do', I see no grounds at all for claiming that 'moral experts' might not exist. Certainly (on some views of moral language) I can without logical inconsistency disagree – I can say something like "Well, whatever you tell me, I am jolly well going to value such-and-such." But what I cannot do is to say this with any show of *reason*. As soon as reason enters into the arena at all, we have to grant that some people will be better placed to grasp and wield it than others.

Various alarmist thoughts need not follow: e.g. that 'moral experts' should have power to enforce their views, or that we are already sufficiently clear (and able to verify) just who these experts are. Nor does it follow that the same 'expert' will be expert in respect of *all* the attributes that make up 'the good moralist' or 'the morally educated person': we might need a whole panel of experts. My thesis has been a more modest one. But if it is correct, it suggests that a good deal more attention should be paid to this expertise (or kinds of different expertises) than has yet been paid to it.

This (as it were) methodological approach, which relies solely on the idea of expertise (rather than proof), must commend itself even to those philosophers (e.g. Hare, 1963) who most want to stress the connection between value on the one hand and choice or personal commitment, 'prescriptiveness', on the other: for even they acknowledge that *some* form of reason is applicable to moral and other choices of value – indeed, the process of reasoning recommended by such philosophers turns out often to be quite complicated (as in 'ideal observer' or 'ideal prescriber' theories: e.g. Hare, 1976). For educational purposes, and generally for anyone concerned (as all must in some contexts be concerned) that a close link is retained between rightness and actual behaviour, views of this kind are very important (Wilson, 1971a, pp. 134ff.). But that does not, in my judgement, go any way at all to show that what is right and wrong, good and bad, desirable and undesirable, for men cannot be regarded as a matter of *fact*, or that there are not *truths* here, as secure as (though of course different in their status and provenance from) other truths that we acknowledge as evident. The strictly logical point, that one cannot move deductively from 'is' to 'ought', tends sometimes to obscure this: but that point comes, on reflection, to seem somewhat bleak and isolated, rather like a house that stands by itself in an otherwise devastated city. For the evaluative or normative input (if we must use such terms) comes from our desire to remain rational creatures or people who have dealings with other people; and this, plus a few other fairly obvious conceptual points, may be enough to give us all that we need. I will offer, very briefly, a few examples of how this might be so.

First, philosophy might help not by specifying the *content* of particular virtues, but rather by keeping their *form* and importance clearly before our minds: ensuring that they are, as it were, permanently on the agenda of human life, even though disputes about their content may continue. This might be thought otiose and useless, on the twin grounds (a) that we have them permanently on the agenda anyway, and (b) that all the important disputes are about their content. But this is not so. What happens only too often is that certain virtues disappear or receive no conscious attention, and others become unduly valued or at least talked about; and this may be far more destructive than the assignation of an improper content. To take a fairly topical example, in many circles the virtues which may be marked by 'chastity' and 'obedience' or ('doing one's duty') are either not considered at all, or dismissed as virtues because of their associations with an improper and obsolete content: 'chastity' is construed as consisting of supposedly absurd sexual prohibitions, or 'obedience' as connoting some kind of blind conformity to irrational authority. But it is clear enough that all human beings must have, and therefore ought to reflect upon the contents of, some kind of physical or

semi-physical self-concept, an image of the good or uncorrupted (undefiled) self, counterposed to the idea of invasion or
corruption or defilement from external sources; and, even
more obviously, the concepts marked by 'authority', 'obedience', 'duty' and other cognate notions are written into almost
any form of joint human endeavour.

Secondly, it is arguable that rational creatures require some
minimal form of parenting or some minimal society for their
continued existence; and whether this is so or not, the existence of some (any) society may be taken as a starting-point for
all those who do not want to, or cannot, be hermits. We can
then show that any social group necessitates such norms as
truth-telling (otherwise how could the individuals communicate effectively?) (Winch, 1972), some kind of adjudicating
procedure or justice (otherwise the individuals could not do
business together), protection for the liberty of the individual
(since liberty to achieve one's ends goes along with the idea
that one wants to achieve them), and so forth. There are many
items one can add in here, with interesting results, such as
some minimal and inexpellable notion of property (if only the
undisturbed use of one's own body), and in particular the
constellation of concepts marked by 'authority', 'punishment'
and other terms, about which I have written more fully elsewhere (Wilson, 1977).

Thirdly, there are goods for both individuals and society
(though different for each, to some extent) not all of which are
moral virtues, or even virtues at all. One thinks of such things
as power, invulnerability, intelligence, good communications,
the use of one's physical organs, freedom from pain, beauty,
and many others. We often tend to overlook these because we
take them for granted: but it is difficult to imagine any serious
political or moral discussion (meaning, here, discussion about
a society or an individual) which did not rely on their desirability. The desirability follows, in some cases obviously if in
some less so, from the simple notions of a rational creature and
a social group. How, for instance, could anyone think that
communication in a society ought characteristically to be bad –
since part of what we mean by a society is a number of
individuals who sometimes act collectively and hence need to
know what other people think? Of course there would sometimes be a case for closing down communications, e.g. for the

sake of secrecy in wartime; but that would relate to another indisputable good, such as survival, and could not characteristically or normally hold. At the very least it would be in principle a good, something any sensible society would be aware of as desirable unless outweighed by very severe disadvantages.

Fourthly, there are the goods we take on board when we have, and to the extent that we have, committed ourselves to *particular* practical enterprises: for then we work within certain fixed parameters. Much moral and political philosophy has overlooked the very obvious fact that questions of value often, indeed nearly always, arise within some such enterprise, not in an entirely abstract and context-free way – and that fact is important, even though there are not a few (sometimes agonising) cases which are of a more general, enterprise-free kind. Whilst there are indeed questions about whether one ought to be a good citizen of one's country, or go in for education, or stay married, there are also (and more usually) questions about how to be a good citizen, or how to educate well, or how to improve one's marriage. Here, as I have shown at length in the case of education (Wilson, 1979a), the limits are clearly laid down by the concepts which mark out the enterprises. I shall discuss this particular point later and will go no further here.

Ordinary people expect philosophers to tell them how to live, or at least to tell them what the most important things in life are. They are quite right to expect this, and one of the disasters of recent analytic philosophy has been that it has not only failed to tell them what they expected but also told them that they were wrong to expect it. It is also a piece of irony bordering on the tragic that, at more or less the same time as philosophers appreciated the importance of analytic methodology and thus (perhaps for the first time in history) gained a position from which they had a good chance of giving ordinary people some correct answers based on solid reasoning, they insisted on denying themselves the right to do this. Various reasons may be given for this self-imposed impotence, but the failure is all the more peculiar in that a good many elements in the general spirit of analytic philosophy – particularly what might be described as a common-sense, workmanlike, unheated, uninflated and down-to-earth approach, perhaps as much to do with the temperament of its practitioners as with what they practice – seem to lend themselves naturally to the kind of work required. For the first (in a sense, the only) thing to be said is that we must look for the answers not in particular creeds or ideologies, but in certain general values or other characteristics that are not the unique property of any one -ism. The point is transparently obvious and in no way sophisticated. We know well enough, when we keep our heads, that what makes a good parent, or a good marriage, or a good school, or a good friendship, or a good government, or even a good social occasion is not anything ideological, or doctrinal, or (in one sense at least) theoretical. We know that there are commendable examples of all these which do not have any ideological common ground: they have common ground, but not of that sort. Not are we totally at a loss when trying to describe what that ground consists of. We have, in fact, quite good ideas both of what counts as being a reasonable or even a good man in general, and of what counts as being reasonable in, or good at, various particular enterprises. These ideas derive, again quite understandably, from two basic sources: (1) an intuitive grasp of the difference between reasonable and unreasonable or non-reasonable postures or attitudes or procedures, and (2) an intuitive grasp of the inalienable elements or necessary features of human nature. We shall have more to say about these later (Chapter 3).

(C) 'ORDINARY LANGUAGE'

I conclude this chapter with some (very brief) remarks on this topic, for two reasons: first, because of the close association of phrases like 'ordinary language', 'normal usage' and others with conceptual analysis; and second, because even a cursory consideration points us in a direction similar to that which other considerations have already suggested to us.

What sort of association is this, though? For instance, is it just a contingent or historical association – is it perhaps just that certain philosophers in Oxford and Cambridge happened at a certain time to be interested in ordinary language? Or is there some methodological connection, in that anyone interested in exhibiting conceptual implications for philosophical purposes would do well to attend to ordinary language? Or, more strongly, a logical or necessary connection, in that such a person must necessarily pay such attention? And what are we to make of the phrase 'ordinary language' anyway? The contingent and historical connections are not without interest, and give us some kind of lead in attempting to say what might be meant by 'ordinary language'. The most obvious of such connections is with the name and work of Austin, perhaps the ablest and most influential philosopher in this genre; and here a number of very striking facts obtrude themselves. First, as his closest (or most devout) associates are constantly obliged to point out, Austin himself nowhere *states* anything that could seriously be described as a 'thesis' or 'theory' about philosophical method or philosophy itself: his own private notes make very modest and strictly limited claims, presenting a methodological profile so low as to be almost invisible (and one which stands in the sharpest contrast to his own very powerful personal presence and very considerable influence). Secondly, however (and perhaps this could in fact be called a 'thesis' or 'theory' about philosophical *method*, or one philosophical method, even if the content of such a thesis is of a different order from the more substantive recipes of some philosophers), he did believe in and practise, with great consistency and insistence, certain virtues and procedures in his own philosophical enquiries: including an intense passion for clarity, accuracy and the eliciting of fine distinctions in 'ordinary language'. His methodology was, in fact, extremely distinctive: and the passion which informed it argues, if not for a 'thesis', at least for a very strong belief that it was worth pursuing.

In this light a third fact appears as striking: that he nowhere gives any very clear account of what 'ordinary language' is supposed to *be*. Urmson (1969, pp. 80–1) says this in a footnote to 'ordinary language' (as against 'the distinctions which *philosophers* thought up in their studies and employed'):

Here, as commonly among Austin and his associates, 'ordinary' is a technical term, meaning 'non-philosophical'; thus the terms of modern physics are for present purposes part of ordinary language. The term is unfortunate because it is also

true that Austin investigated mainly the resources of ordinary ('everyday', 'non-technical') as opposed to technical
language . . .

and goes on to talk of 'scientists and other technical people'.
But this raises a whole host of questions and difficulties, most
of which arise because either (a) we shall adopt a very wide
meaning for 'philosophical' and 'technical' such that almost
any term (or almost any term of any interest) can come under
these headings, or else (b) we adopt narrower meanings, in
which case many terms will pass through the kind of sieve we
seem to want to use. Consider, for instance, the terms 'God',
'the dictatorship of the proletariat', 'neurotic', 'role', 'self-
starter' and many others: is it at all clear which of these are
'philosophical' or 'technical' language and which are not? If
(a), all: if (b), none. The apparent equation of 'everyday' with
'non-technical' is as unclear as the other equation of 'everyday'
with 'non-philosophical': what one hears 'every day', in pubs
or cafés or wherever, depends on what sort of society one lives
in (particularly, here, whether it goes in for philosophy – or,
not here distinguished, ideology – or technology).

Ryle (1963) claims two distinct senses of 'ordinary': one in
which he contrasts it with " . . . 'out-of-the-way', 'esoteric',
'technical', 'poetical' " and others: the other in which "It is not
in contrast with 'esoteric', 'archaic' or 'specialist', etc. It is in
contrast with 'non-stock' or 'non-standard' " (pp. 108–9). The
trouble with this is that a word can be 'non-stock' *by* being
'technical', 'esoteric', etc.: as Ryle appears tacitly to admit
when he says later that "non-stock uses of a word are, e.g.,
metaphorical, hyperbolical, poetical" (the term 'poetical' appears in both of his contrasts). Nevertheless the distinction
would hold provided we could distinguish reasonably well
between the ordinary (in Ryle's first sense) and the specialised.
But we can do this only if we think that there are *some* kinds of
discourse which are not 'specialised', in the sense that they are
(by and large) not *avoidable* by normal human beings: they are
not the special preserve of those with particular and optional
interests in (for instance) religion, or ideology, or natural
science, or the arts and crafts, or any other activity which a
man might or might not take up. (Which these are, and the
criteria by which they are to be identified, would of course be

matters of dispute.) That would go along with the idea that in these areas at least there is likely to be, not only (as Austin did claim) a rich set of distinctions and concepts which it will be useful for conceptual analysis to understand, but also – since all or nearly all men will, *ex hypothesi*, have been doing business and communicating with each other for many years – a good deal more clarity and a good deal less obscurity and incoherence than *may* exist in *some* other areas of discourse.

These two ideas, in themselves perhaps plausible even in advance of argument, would help to account for the fact that it is possible to agree about 'what we would say' in cases where ordinary (i.e. non-specialised) language is involved: for, again *ex hypothesi*, we have all learned the rules for such language at our mothers' knees and been able to apply them successfully, if unconsciously, in talking and listening to our fellow men. By contrast, if we were asked 'what we would say' in some more specialised area of, say, science or ideology, then either we might be ignorant and not know what to say, or else we might say very different things from each other because of our different outlooks.

This in turn suggests, what I take to be central to the importance of 'ordinary language' and at the same time to be much more in dispute, the idea that we can draw some sort of distinction between discourse which is free from specialist, or ideological, or theoretical commitments on the one hand and discourse which is to some extent theory-laden on the other. Such a distinction must be possible, because (briefly) we could not have the concept marked by 'theory' (or some such term) unless it could be contrasted with the non-theoretical. The main point, however, is not that whole tracts of discourse are held to be totally free from theory – no doubt the rules governing such tracts look always to some object or purpose, or reflect some specific concern (if that is enough, as I think it is not, to justify the term 'theory'). It is rather, as we said earlier, that some features of human life and some human concerns are inexpellable or inalienable; so that the 'ordinary language' and concepts which deal with these features and concerns are, as it were, given. In *that* sense (and in that alone) 'ordinary language' may indeed be thought to have, not so much a special authority, but a special (because central) interest.

However, this idea jumps a number of guns. In particular it

not only assumes that there are such central and inexpellable features, but also that these will in fact be conceptualised by human beings and marked in ('ordinary') language. Both of these notions have in fact been strongly denied in recent philosophical thinking. It has been supposed that the world (to put it briefly) is very much what we make it or conceptualise it as, rather than given in any absolute way: that human concepts or conceptualisations are historical and time-bound entities, which constantly change, and reflect diverse and changing human interests: and hence that, although 'ordinary language' may be a useful – perhaps, since we all speak it, an inevitable – place to start, there is no special reason to regard it as either authoritative in itself or as offering us any uniquely reliable or authoritative guide to the nature of reality. In order to meet such difficulties, we need to look more closely at certain notions – in particular the notion of a *concept*. This will be our concern in the next chapter.

2 Concepts and Contestability

There is, I believe, one central reason both why conceptual analysts may have been unduly timid and retiring in their response to the plain man's demands, and why philosophical fashion has turned, or is turning, away from conceptual analysis. It is that there has never been any agreement, or any well-clarified and well-publicised agreement, about concepts; even though that term must be more used than almost any other in the present context. Consequently there now exists in some circles (fairly near, as I see it, to the centre of the Inferno) something rather too fuzzy to be called a set of doctrines, but rather too specific – and articulated by too many intelligent people – to be too quickly dismissed as a mere fashion or climate of opinion. It seems to involve (1) a general view of what concepts are, and hence of the limitations or dangers of conceptual analysis, and (2) a slightly more specific view about certain concepts, namely that they are 'contestable' or 'essentially contestable'.

Nearly all the literature seems either (at worst) simply to *adopt* these views, or (at best) to assume that we are sufficiently clear about the nature of concepts to be able to see the point and criticise the practice of conceptual analysis, and to speak clearly about the existence of 'contestable concepts'. For my part I am not so optimistic. Hence, though I shall refer to certain pieces of literature, I am obliged to begin where the beginning ought to be and make a few points – often in reaction to what is said in the literature – about the nature of concepts. In this I follow Frege (1950) (and ultimately Plato), but hope to add something to his account, or at least to clarify some points for the modern reader.

'Concept' is clearly a term of art: though, since like other such terms ('role', 'neurotic', 'motivation') it has made a fairly successful invasion of everyday speech, not much may be gained in trying to pin it down by the usual techniques of analysis. It is often used as a pseudo-professional or scientific-sounding alternative for the still common term 'idea', and for that reason used mostly in rather high-minded talk: "His idea of a party is for everyone to get drunk as quickly as possible" is natural, whereas "His concept of a party . . ." is a little precious; on the other hand "The Russians' concept of democracy is different from ours" is wholly acceptable. These and similar examples arouse the suspicion – well-founded, as I hope to show – that 'concept' is a kind of uneasy half-way house between the notion of some kind of mental entity or structure on the one hand, and the notion of the meaning of words on the other. The unease is displayed by the indecisiveness of philosophers about whether to write "the concept of democracy" or "the concept of 'democracy' ": both usages are common.

It is significant that only certain candidates seem allowable in filling out "the concept of X". Admittedly, in the high and palmy days of linguistic analysis, articles appeared with such titles as "The Concept of 'Of' "; but characteristically at least it was and is only *nouns* or noun-phrases that should apply. We talk of the meaning of 'and', 'slowly', 'walked', and 'red': if we insisted on using 'concept' we should slide naturally into talking of slowness, or walking (a gerund), or redness ('the red'). There is an important exception to this in proper names: no one talks of the concept of Adolf Hitler, though titles are acceptable ('the concept of the Fuehrer'). This may perhaps be because with proper names there is no question of identifying or recognising *cases* of the same kind, since there is only one such case. But anyway we talk as if there were a number of *things* in the world of various kinds – physical objects, acts, processes, activities and so forth – and as if we had, or failed to have, some kind of mental grasp, idea, conception or concept of these things; and this seems rather different from (though of course it is connected with) our understanding of how to use a language, since we understand how to use 'and', 'slowly', etc. but have no temptation to say that we have 'the concept of' them. (Of what? What would 'them' refer to?)

So far, perhaps, so good. But at this point most philosophers make some sort of distinction between what might be called the psychological sense of 'concept', whereby it can include one's private associations ("My concept of a German is a blond beast in jackboots"), and a sense which is tied, or more tied, to the notion of rules of meaning. In this second sense 'to have the concept X' will be roughly equivalent to 'to understand (not necessarily to be able to articulate) the rules governing the term "X" ', and perhaps to be able to pick out cases of X in the world (Wilson, 1972, pp. 72ff.). That is, I think, an entirely reasonable distinction; and we say quite naturally that, for instance, someone "doesn't know what 'check-mate' means", or (more loosely) "doesn't know what check-mate is", or (more technically) "doesn't have the concept of check-mate". We shall note also that a term X may share the same rules of meaning as a term Y, either within the same natural language (as a synonym) or from two or more languages: so that the same concept is marked by 'dog', 'chien' and 'Hund', concepts being related to words in much the same way as propositions are related to sentences. All that is, or used to be, common ground; but it is also, I shall argue, rather uncertain ground.

The uncertainty arises because of a tension between two ideas. The first idea, very obvious in psychological uses of 'concept', is that if I have a concept then I *have* something (in my head, as it were), some kind of *possession*, rather like having the crown jewels in my pocket. We then find ourselves talking naturally of 'my' ('your', 'his', etc.) concept, as if a concept were a sort of image or echo of the thing which it is a concept of. Notoriously philosophers in the last few decades have reacted against this idea in favour of the second idea; which is, roughly, that if I have a concept I do not have any kind of private possession, but rather stand in some kind of relation to something: like having a view of the sea rather than the crown jewels. Then we talk more easily of *the* concept or *the* thing or *the* meaning of certain words: 'the concept of check-mate', 'check-mate', 'the meaning of "check-mate" '. But now we are talking as if concepts live and move and have their being independently of men, or independently at least of this or that man: they are in some sense *there*, whether or not individuals or societies latch onto them – as if there is something called 'check-mate' whether or not people play chess.

This worries us because (we feel) concepts and meaning, if not things (or at least some things), must surely be human creations, man-made and – as some will be very quick to say – 'the product of society'. So then we revert to the first idea of a concept as some kind of possession.

However, this worry is unnecessary. Men can create things without owning them. It seems implausible to say that check-mate, or the concept of check-mate, is somehow eternally hanging about, waiting for men to understand it; but it is equally implausible to talk of check-mate as a possession, even though its existence was the result of human invention. 'My' ('your', etc.) 'concept of check-mate' makes no sense: nor, I shall argue, does any possessive pronoun placed before 'concept of X' make sense. Men distinguish or categorise the world in various ways, encapsulating bits of it in various sets of rules: the distinctions, or categories, or sets of rules, or ranges of meaning, are referred to in shorthand by the term 'concept'. Characteristically these are marked by certain terms in natural languages; and the correct usage, rarely followed by philosophers, is in full "The concept (range of meaning) marked, in twentieth-century English, by the word 'check-mate' " (plus, if needed, further specifications about the English-speakers and the contexts in which the term is used).

"But surely we can have different concepts of the same thing: so that we can intelligibly, as Hirst and Peters (amongst many others) say, ask and answer the question 'Whose concept are you analysing?' " (Hirst and Peters, 1970, p. 8). Well, what could it mean to talk of 'my concept of check-mate' or 'his concept of democracy' – remembering, of course, that we have excluded the psychological sense of 'concept' and are ruling out private associations as irrelevant? The only possibility is that I mean something different by 'check-mate' from what is normally meant: but why should that be described as 'my concept of check-mate'? I have no doubt a concept of some kind, and mark it by the term 'check-mate': but that is not good enough. What I entertain or stand in relation to is a different concept and a different thing (perhaps, for instance, what most of us mean by 'check'): it is not a concept *of* *check-mate* at all. The fact that I may use the same word is neither here nor there. Nobody (I hope) wants to say that across the English Channel people 'have a different concept of chat', just because the French use the word 'chat' to mean an animal and the English to mean a talk. Of course it would be possible to ask *which* concept one was analysing, if all that had happened was that someone had mentioned a word that marked more than one concept, like 'chat'; and one might, I suppose, mean this (rather perversely) by asking whose concept one was analysing. ("I am analysing the concept of mass." "Whose concept, the physicists' or the Roman Catholics'?"). But as soon as the concept has been identified, there is no more room for the possessive pronoun.

"But can I not invent my own concepts – would not those at least be personal possessions?" Certainly I can do this: I can, for instance, put together some features of girls by the criterion of what I happen to find attractive, and invent a word for someone who has all these features: "I like squiggly girls." But 'my concept of squiggly girls' will still make no sense; for it suggests that other people might have their concept of squiggly girls, and though other people of course have their concept of what girls they find attractive, that is not a concept of *squiggly* girls. There is, simply *the* concept of squiggly girls (the range of meaning marked by 'squiggly girls'): one which perhaps only I and a few friends share, but whose status and nature in no way depends logically upon the fact that I invented it. 'Squiggly', if it is a genuinely meaningful word, is in principle a word in a public language, able to be explained to others: and the concept goes along with that.

"But all this is a fuss about nothing: when we talk of 'my' ('his', etc.) 'concept of X' or about the concept of X being contestable we mean simply that the verbal markers cover different ground for different people. A means one thing by 'democracy', B another; and often they fight about it." It is nothing new that different people mean different things by the same word; but what we should say here is that the word marks different concepts, not (repeat *not*) that one and the same concept is being contested. Indeed I do not see, despite having soused myself to the point of drunkenness in the literature, what could be meant by contesting a *concept*. Provided one knew what the concept was, what range of meaning or set of rules we were talking about, what is there to contest? How can one contest a range of meaning? Ranges of meaning are what they are: of course one can argue about what they are, but that is the usual kind of philosophical argument with which we are all familiar.

What else can one argue about or contest? So far as I can see, there are only the following candidates:

(1) We can argue about whether some particular instance does or does not in point of fact fall within a particular concept. Thus, if (which I do not believe) 'education' may reasonably be taken to mark a concept one of the rules of which is evaluative – that is, if something only counts as education when that something is a good thing – then we may of course argue about whether this or that classroom period counts as education, the argument turning partly on whether the period does good or harm or neither. But that is no more a case of contesting the *concept* of education than moral or other evaluative arguments are cases of contesting the concept of goodness. 'Good' means whatever it does mean: what particular items we should call good is another matter.

(2) We can argue – and, as I shall say later, this sort of argument is very important – about what concepts we need to have or pay heed to. Such arguments should surely at least begin with getting clear about the concepts we actually do have: that is, those actually marked by highly visible (and hence readily intelligible) groups of language-users in various parts of the world at various times (not just twentieth-century English). But they need not end there: not just because (though this has been the point generally seized on) some terms do not guide us, even after exhaustive analysis, to fairly clear-cut concepts, but more obviously and directly because the mere existence of a concept is not in itself an overwhelming argument for its importance.

So far as I can see (and I speak with some hesitation), almost everything said in the literature can be reduced to one or other of these matters. Gallie, *fons et origo mali*, for instance says that "We find groups of people disagreeing about *the proper use of the concepts* e.g. of art, of democracy, of the Christian tradition", and almost immediately continues "Different *uses of the term* 'work of art' or 'democracy' or 'Christian doctrine' . . ." (my italics) (Gallie, 1956, pp. 167–98). But only the most tolerant of interpretations could render this even intelligible. If there are different uses of a term X, then we have different ranges of meaning and so different concepts: what then can be meant by talking of 'the proper use of the concepts'? The whole idea of 'using a concept properly' (or improperly) is incoherent: to 'use' a concept, if it means anything, presumably means that we bring it to bear on a particular case (we 'use' the concept of check-mate in identifying cases of check-mate); and if I apply some other set of rules to the situation (say, the rules marked by 'check') I have no dealings with the concept of check-mate at all.

To take another example, the criticisms of 'conceptual analysis' in reference to education advanced by Hartnett and Naish (1976, pp. 99ff.) rest on the same confusion. "Different individuals and social groups may *use concepts differently*": and concepts do not occupy more or less fixed positions – there is rather a 'flexibility and fluidity of use'. "Thus we might argue that 'What is education?' is a request for a programmatic definition . . . to be defended not merely by considerations of consistency and clarity but also by normative ones – concerning, for example, the worth of the programme . . . ." But if there are, as the authors more reasonably say (more reasonably, because they are now talking about the *words*), "a number of different and competing uses of 'education' or 'educated' ", then we should simply say that these terms are ambiguous or multifarious – that people mean different things by them and have different concepts. Any serious attempt to offer a *definition* could not be, in the authors' sense, 'programmatic': for to offer a definition *means* (in ordinary English, and if the authors are speaking another language they should warn us to that effect) to take account of the uses of a term as we find them, not as we would like them to be. ("My definition of 'religion' is 'a load of rubbish' " will not do, however correctly atheistical the speaker, because 'religion' just doesn't mean that.) The authors might have said (and get near to saying, sometimes) that 'education' means something like 'a programme of learning favoured by the speaker' – that would at least be a shot at a definition. (Although a very bad shot: it is perfectly good sense to say that it is wrong to educate such-and-such a person. We speak of bad – not just incompetent – education, just as we speak of bad religion, bad morality and

bad politics. The most natural dividing-lines of these enterprises are *not* given to us by our own educational, religious,
moral or political values.)

I hope it is not labouring the points unduly to quote a further
example in the same field. Ryan (1974) in a review of Richard
Peters' work on education speaks of education as

> an essentially contested concept – one whose meaning [*sic*] is
> up for grabs so long as people want to emphasise the import-
> ance of different aspects of the extended family of activities
> which people associate with education.

I find this largely unintelligible as it stands; a kindly translation
is needed to make sense of it at all. The phrase 'one whose
meaning' implies that concepts somehow *have* meaning (instead of themselves being certain ranges of meaning): I suppose by 'concept' he must mean 'word'. Then we are told that
there are 'activities which people associate with education':
this might be intelligible in itself if he meant 'activities associated with the actual business of education' – for instance, the
activity of financing it, sitting in classrooms, and so on; and I
suppose some 'associations' might be more idiosyncratic, as
one might say "I always associate education with the smell of
cabbage and inkpots." Since this seems to have absolutely
nothing to do with concepts in any philosophical sense of the
term, I suspect he means ' . . . associate with "education" ',
since the term 'education' has something to do with meaning,
whereas the actual real-life business of education does not. But
now 'associate' is still very odd: one might have all sorts of
associations connected with a word ("I always associate the
word 'catamaran' with meringues"), which had nothing to do
with its meaning. Perhaps he means ' . . . activities which
people count as part of the meaning of "education" ', but this
is still not quite right, since an activity cannot count as part of
any meaning. Let us try ' . . . activities whose descriptions
count as part of the meaning of "education" ' (as one might
think that the activity we describe as 'learning' was part of what
we meant by 'education'). But now we have moved from
association to meaning, and either such an item *is* part of the
meaning or it is not.

At the risk of being tedious, I should like to make my

position clearer by considering the idea that concepts have histories. This seems to be very widely believed; many philosophers say boldly (as Williams in Magee, 1978) that all concepts have a history, and claim that neglect of this fact was an important defect of 'linguistic analysis' a decade or so ago. But if we consider just *what* is supposed to have a history, we may be less bold. Not, presumably, concepts in the psychological, sublunary sense of 'ideas', as when we say "Our idea of feminine beauty has changed since the Victorian age" and employ historians to trace the change and its causes. What then? Our understanding of the phrase 'feminine beauty'? But *prima facie* that understanding has not changed: it seems likely that the Victorians would have translated those words much as we would now translate them. Very well: suppose they would have translated them differently. Then the phrase 'feminine beauty' meant something different then from what it does now; in other words, we have another concept. It is not the *concept* that has changed, but *us*. Probably the phrase meant the same to the Victorians as to us, but we accept different instances from the ones they accept: and there is nothing mysterious about this, any more than there is about the fact that we have a different range of useful medicines from the range they had – the concept marked by 'useful medicine' has not changed.

If we talk of history or change at all in relation to concepts (and I incline with Frege to think that, strictly speaking, we ought not – any more than we should talk of them in relation to mathematical entities), it will be talk about how particular groups of men stood in relation to certain ranges of meaning – just as the history of mathematics is not, I take it, the history of the number seven or of triangles, but the history of human understanding of these things. It is even arguable – though not a question I wish to pursue – whether we really ought to say that concepts depend for their existence entirely upon men: that they are created when men create them, and die when they have no more use for them. For if we talk, as we do, of grasping or understanding or learning a concept, then in some sense the concept must exist outside our grasping or understanding or learning: just as we would not talk of human beings (even if they were all colour-blind) coming to be able to distinguish between green and red if we did not think that in some sense green and red were just *there* to be distinguished.

Part of the trouble here is, as with the case of colours, that once we *mention* a concept (in language) then provided we know what we are talking about we already entertain it. Consider the case of 'scrawlie', a term used by some children to cover anything that could be written on by crayons (paper, walls, etc.). These children, let us say, are now dead or have forgotten their early conceptual furniture: and we raise the question "Is there such a thing as the concept of a scrawlie?" I think we should be inclined to say 'yes' rather than 'no': there is such a thing, a range of meaning we can mark, whether or not anyone now marks it. Do we say that pre-scientific ages did not grasp the concept of (say) gravity, or that there was no concept of gravity for them to grasp? Again, I think the former. But nothing very substantial seems to turn on which move we make here. Suppose someone wanted to argue that 'concept' ought properly to refer to a range of meaning only as grasped by a person or persons – since after all the root-meaning of the word, and the word's history, do point in that direction: then it will be necessary to find another term to refer to ranges of meaning whether or not they are grasped. The choice is rather like that which we might have to make with a term like 'wealth'. We might want to restrict the term only to what was actually owned and enjoyed by someone; or we might want to say that there was, in a wider and different sense, 'wealth' or 'treasure' even if not actually owned or immediately available, so long as it was available in principle – if it were at the bottom of the sea, for instance. In fact we do use 'wealth' in both ways; and I suppose we might use 'concept' in both ways too, though we should need to be clear about the difference. I raise these points, only to show that it is possible to take a very different view of concepts than the one which seems currently fashionable: a view to which, perhaps, we are driven once we begin to distinguish clearly between concepts, our grasp of concepts, our identification of cases falling within concepts, and our general pictures, preferences or ideas about the world.

"But surely, if 'the concept of X' is equivalent to 'the range of meaning marked by the term "X" ', then concepts do change: for the meaning which such markers mark can, indeed almost certainly will, vary in different regions of space and time." Yes: but nobody in his senses would make *that* equivalence: it would land him with saying that the term 'chat' represented a single concept – but what? The concept of a domestic animal or of a casual conversation? We have to add " . . . the term 'X' as used by such-and-such speakers at such-and-such a time", and perhaps more besides (the context in which the term is used, for instance). But now this addition will have specified a particular concept which does not change but is simply what it is. To take another example, suppose that I wave a wand and the term 'No' is substituted for the term 'Yes', and vice versa, on all occasions. The meaning of the words has changed completely: but does anyone want to say that any *concepts* have changed? Surely not: we should say, perhaps, that the 'concept of affirmation' (or denial) is what it always has been (how could that sort of thing alter?): and bringing in the words 'affirmation' and 'denial' would be an attempt to get behind the changes and chances of word-usage so as to make this point.

Thus so far as the concept of education goes, I have argued elsewhere (Wilson, 1979a) that there is an enterprise, normally marked by 'education' in twentieth-century English and by parallel terms in most languages, of which the defining characteristics are (1) that it aims to promote learning above the level of nature, (2) that it is conducted intentionally, (3) that the learning is of a fairly long-term, systematic and sustained character, and (4) that it is directed at, or for the benefit of, people as such, taking all or most of the important aspects of a person into consideration. (I have also argued that this concept, so outlined, is one we not only need but cannot well imagine ourselves without; but that is another issue, which I shall take up later on.) In other words, I think it is simply false that the concept of education is contestable, even if those words could be given any clear sense: there is something which can fairly be called *the* concept of education. Whether I am right about what it is does not matter so much: what matters, methodologically, is that we should reach agreement about whether this is so or not. Obviously we cannot reach such agreement without a good deal more, and more careful, conceptual analysis than has been done so far (that some suggested analyses are objectionable is not a good reason for giving up the whole business). This policy, which seems the only sane one whatever one may think about contestable concepts, is not well served by those philosophers who appear to assume, in advance of the work that needs to be done, that the work is not worth doing or will yield little profit.

In this connection, and because it seems important that conceptual analysis should be understood for what it is, perhaps a few (necessarily brief and therefore rather over-crisp) comments on what Hartnett and Naish say may be in order: all the more since, as I would guess, they are fairly representative of some popular misunderstandings:

(1) " . . . when we are asked to make a map of an area, its boundaries can be sharply defined . . . . But can the area marked out by every concept be similarly . . . delimited?" Of course not all concepts are sharply defined: there are borderline cases, cases where we may have to make a strategic decision rather than give a right answer, and cases which may make us revise our ideas quite radically. But neither are areas sharply defined: the Isle of Wight may be (though what about the Needles?), but the Sahara is not.

(2) " . . . the logical area *marked out by* a concept is that determined by all *its uses* . . . . But how are we to know that our collection of *uses* is not selective?" What I have italicised makes no sense: the substitution of 'word' for 'concept' is required. And of course our 'collection' *is* 'selective': we look at 'chat' in twentieth-century English, not French. We – that is, the 'we' who are reading these words – do best to start at least with twentieth-century English simply because we are most familiar with it: but nothing prevents our doing the same thing with classical Greek or ancient Sanskrit.

(3) " . . . do all *concepts have uses* [*sic*] which can be indisputably identified as central, primary, and paradigm . . . . Further, by what criteria are such uses identified?" Fair questions: the answer to the first is plainly 'No' (assuming that by 'concepts' they mean 'words'), but what of it? The answer to the second is more difficult; but if someone were to maintain, for instance, that the use of the adverb 'religiously', or the phrase 'law of the jungle', was absolutely central to our understanding of the concepts marked by 'religion' and 'law', not only I but I think even Hartnett and Naish would think that such a person did

not know much English. The fact is, we do identify
central cases: we could not speak of metaphors or daring
usages or other such if we did not.

(4) In arguing for some kind of historical rather than logical
enquiry, they say " . . . what sort of understanding could
be had of 'work of art', without reference to the history
of art and to the debates about art in which the concept
had a place?" Well, quite a lot of understanding: is it
supposed that those of us who are not up in this history
and these debates do *not* understand what 'work of art'
means – or even that a reasonably intelligent child might
not understand? We say to him (I do not attempt a full
definition) something like "No, this thing isn't supposed
to be any *use*, it's just meant to look pretty/sound excit-
ing/give you a special kind of pleasure/be an interesting
story: and somebody's created it, probably for that reason". What is so mysterious about that? There are indeed
mysteries about art, but not all of them are about the
concept.

(5) . . . to interpret 'What is education?' as a demand for
logical geography may be false to the most typical
contexts in which such a question is asked. It might be
argued that its home is not in philosophical seminars
where it appears, like a body left to medical science,
chilled and ready for dissection, but in discussions by
interested parties about what to teach in schools,
colleges and universities. If this is true, the argument
about the nature of education is taken most naturally
as a normative one.

I quote this purple passage at length because it strikes at
the root of the whole practice of conceptual analysis. The
authors may well be quite right – it is, I suppose, an
empirical question – in saying that when many people
ask "What is education?" they really mean (and surely
this is the proper way of putting it) "What ought our
educational system to consist of?"; and they are certainly
right in saying that "questions of the form 'What is X?'
may be understood in many different ways". We learned
this at our tutor's knee when we realised that Socrates

and Thrasymachus were doing two different things with
the question "What is justice?" in Book I of the *Republic*. Yes: but *one* of the ways – the philosophical way
– of taking the question is "What do we, or might we, or
would we be best advised to, take as the meaning of the
term 'education'? What are we going to talk about under
this heading – what shall we take the category-title to
include?" And to answer *this* question we need, if not
the chill atmosphere of the dissecting-room, at least an
atmosphere freed from the norms and values that interested parties wish to promote – and freed also from
matters of contingent sociological fact (it may be that
religion has been used like opium, but that will not help
us to determine what to count as religion).

I turn now to the perhaps more interesting and certainly more
difficult question of what is to be done when a term marks no
one clear range of meaning: but there are some important
preliminary points to be made. (i) First, I think it unlikely that
there are many such terms: either (a) the term marks a number
of different ranges of meaning – ranges that are still clear, as in
the case of words which are simply ambiguous, or (b) *we* are
not clear what the range of meaning actually is, since we have
not taken the trouble to analyse adequately. Thus before
generalising, we should make a stern effort to look at how we
(whoever 'we' may be) actually use such terms as 'politics',
'morality', 'work of art', 'democracy' and so on – considering
of course, not just these words in themselves but the use of
such phrases as 'a political reason', 'an aesthetic merit', 'morally good', etc. I have not seen this done: certainly not done by
those philosophers who are quick to claim the concepts as
contestable. (ii) Secondly, if and when we feel justifiably
certain that some terms are in some very deep way obscure in
their use, we shall not feel particularly surprised that much
(perhaps most) of the obscurity seems to be contingently
connected with certain human passions or enthusiastic commitments, or that disputes involving such terms continue even
when we appreciate the variety of their use. For we know well
enough that men distort or forget the nature even of clear
concepts in the interests of passion.
This last point, though obvious enough, has perhaps not

been given sufficient weight in relation to the notion of contestable concepts. Some categories and some terms, however obscure their ranges of meaning may be, are at least prestigious or magnetic. Hence, whether or not there is what Gallie calls 'an original exemplar' (as for Christianity and Marxism), there will always be motives – not necessarily justifications – for trying to get one's preferred items under these rather than other categories: thus if I feel strongly about X, I may try (in certain cultures where the category 'moral' cuts more ice than the category 'aesthetic') to get X classified as a moral rather than an aesthetic matter, a matter of taste. The motives may be more or less high-minded: I may want something classified as a work of art simply because that classification will get me a grant from the Arts Council, or (as my *Daily Mirror* reports) to persuade the manager that a black tie and black underwear count as evening dress because I want to display myself in a conventional night-club. Characteristically, however, the temptations are more ideological in nature: people will attempt to force or smuggle their preferred ideologies into certain categories under some disguise or other. 'True' or 'real' education, Plato tells us (*Laws,* 643–4), is learning how to rule or be ruled: the rest does not matter, or does not count as education, or does not 'properly' count as education.

It is luminously clear in all such cases – and the history of many branches of philosophy (education is just one example) consists almost entirely of such – that the authors are not even *trying* to recover a or any concept of education from actual usage. That is not the business they are in. They are selling, or expressing, a line. The man reported as saying "When I say religion of course I mean the Christian religion, and when I say the Christian religion of course I mean the Church of England" cannot be plausibly regarded as attempting some kind of translation or analysis of 'religion' or 'the Christian religion'. Equally, when the concept is in fact extremely unclear (so that a person may be correct in his assertion, if only we could agree about the concept in the first place), he may still not be interested in clarifying it: if I assert that eating pork or masturbating are moral issues, my interest is probably not that of trying to get clear (by means of useful philosophical examples) either what does or what ought to count as a moral issue. What I want is that these things should be taken seriously in certain ways, and 'moral' is the nearest word to hang this interest on. (In another situation I might have used 'un-American' or 'counter-revolutionary'.)

But by the same token such people are not in the business of making strategically sensible recommendations about concepts either: so long as the items *they* are interested in count within the category, they are happy. Whatever the criteria of a strategically sensible recommendation may be, they will not reasonably include brute pressure of *this* kind. Just because I am keen on a particular religion, I have no right as a philosopher either to stretch the existing concept of religion beyond what it will bear, or to recommend a revision of our concepts and categories on the grounds that my particular religion will then be made more easily visible or more respectable or more attractive: or, as I have tried to argue, to try and sneak my religion in under the claim that the concept of religion is contestable. I do not deny that people in fact do all of these things: nor that old concepts may be dropped and new ones created under such pressures. I say only that this is not a respectable or useful way to do any serious kind of philosophical business, since we should be yielding our language up to certain interest groups (our own or some other).

"But surely our concepts and categorisations ought to reflect human interests." Yes: but if philosophy is worth anything, it must be partly as providing a rational means of negotiating interests. Philosophy has second-order interests; and if it has no way of distinguishing these from the first-order interests of partisan groups, it ceases to be philosophy and becomes a kind of rarefied ideology. But of course it has a way, or rather various ways. To take a humble analogy, suppose that my wife and I are furnishing a house. There would be various categories or *species boni* under which we would consider how to furnish it: for instance, we might in most decisions be concerned with the cost of various items, or with their appearance, or with whether they were health or safety hazards, or whether they impressed the neighbours or had sentimental or educational value: even perhaps with their moral merits or demerits (obscene pictures) or their political ones (pictures of Lenin). How do we distinguish these categories or concepts? Not, of course, by allocating bits of furniture to each: for the same bit of furniture can be viewed from all or most angles – the same picture can be expensive, ugly, bug-infested, obscene and so on. We distinguish rather by the kinds of *reasons* and (what is, as Plato makes clear, closely connected) the kinds of *goods* in question. We argue for or against including X in our furniture because it costs a month's salary, may make us ill, is top-heavy, degrades the female sex, or tends to subvert the state. Philosophy might help us here (even perhaps in this pedestrian example) in two fairly obvious ways: first, by sharpening up our understanding *within* each category – that is, chiefly, by making us clearer about what counts as a good reason within each; and secondly, by distinguishing clearly amongst the categories, and providing us (if this does not sound too grand) with some kind of sophisticated taxonomy of categories which would include all or most important classes yet separate each class clearly.

Now suppose that we are genuinely confused about some of the categories or concepts we seem to be using. Suppose, to taken an example from a recent publication (Montefiore, 1979), my wife and I count different cases as coming under the category marked by 'moral'; my wife includes cases which do not involve anyone's acting with full knowledge, whereas I exclude these. She includes the Oedipus case, the case of a man who is 'morally dirty' because of 'his involvement in acts . . . which he had been condemned by fate to perform': I take my stand with Aristotle that moral virtue is a disposition involving choice, a *hexis prohairetikē*. Is her view, to use the author's descriptions, "Primitive unhealthy confusion – or a faithful expression of the real moral paradox and tragedy which is always lurking in the world?" Are we to say, as he immediately adds, that "It depends on how the world is seen: it depends on what is meant and understood by the word 'moral'"? And, more important than these questions and supposed ways of answering them (both of which I regard as premature and partisan), how are my wife and I to *negotiate* this sort of situation in a rational manner?

Well, we should start at least – and perhaps in a sense we might also end – by just trying to understand each other. We should note, for instance, the difference between 'choosing to do what (in some sense I knew) was wrong' and 'choosing to do what (in fact, though I did not know it) was wrong'. We might then see whether, in each case, we would attribute words like

'blame', 'responsible', 'fault', 'guilt' and 'remorse'. We might
find (here I sympathise with the author) that (to put it quickly)
it was a basic and inalienable element in the concept of action –
as we have to learn it in our infancy – that I have to connect the
results of what I do, whether or not intended, with my agency:
and that the distinction between intended and unintended
consequences was a later sophistication. 'Guilt' and therefore
'remorse' (rather than just 'regret') seem tied broadly to the
basic notion of 'doing wrong'; and if post-Lutheran or post-
Kantian moralists insist that 'doing wrong' must, if it has this
tie, mean 'doing wrong intentionally', then this just shows that
these moralists have not thought hard enough about some of
the concepts of action and responsibility – or, if they insist on a
narrower meaning of 'guilt' whereby it can arise only from
intentional wrong-doing, that they are speaking a language of
their own. Here, clearly enough, there would be two concepts
of guilt, not one contestable concept. I might come to see that
Oedipus' feelings are not 'primitive, unhealthy confusion' –
indeed if that was my first reaction to them I should be thinking
as a partisan moralist, not as any kind of logical analyst or
psychoanalyst – but rather, given human beings as they inevitably are, inevitable. She would surely come to see that there
was an important difference between acts done in ignorance
and acts done with knowledge. In other words, we should just
try to *lay out* such cases, matching them with the right (that is,
accurate) descriptions, so that we could see what we were
talking about. Any philosophical or psychological gains we
made would precisely *not* be made by any view *in advance*
about 'how the world is seen' or about 'what is meant and
understood by the word "moral" '. The answers to these
questions – how best to see this part of the world, how best to
use 'moral' – would best follow from, and could not sensibly
precede, our investigation.

I do not see how this investigation could be other than either
logical – that is, a consideration of meaning and implications –
or empirically psychological: or some judicious mixture of the
two. Of course the investigation could very easily turn into a
dispute, eristic rather than dialectic, in which we allow our
respective 'commitments', ideologies, or preferred usages (of
'moral' or any other term) to have weight in their own right
simply because they are ours: but that is a kind of paradigm of

unreason. Even if we are talking about which categories (when we have drawn them clearly) are most important, reasons may be adduced: the question, implicit in this example, of what weight to give to the post-Kantian concept of morality framed in terms of a free agent 'made weak by time and fate, yet strong in will', like Tennyson's Ulysses, as against the Greek-tragedy or Augustinian or Freudian concept, according to which human life is partly the prey of dark, nameless and unseen forces, is at least a question that can be argued about. Almost always those who plump strongly for one do so because they deny (consciously or more often unconsciously) the force of the other. But in educating ourselves here, we are not contesting concepts: we are enlarging and refining our experience so as to see what concepts we need. And if at the end of the day, or of the year, or of our lives, we find ourselves saying still "Well, that's just how I see things", at least we can show grace enough not to pass that off on our pupils or children as if it were a piece of reasonable methodology.

3 Conceptual Necessity

I return the reader again to the two expectations, mentioned at the beginning of Chapter 1, that people have of the philosopher: that he will tell them something about (1) what there is, and (2) how to conduct their lives. The suggestion is, very briefly, that he can meet these demands (a) by showing them what things and concepts they are, as people or human beings, necessarily landed with, and (b) by showing them what it means to conduct practical enterprises well.

That is not only excessively vague, but in at least one important way misleading: (a) and (b) do not mark an adequate distinction. For part of (b), showing people what it means to perform well at certain practical enterprises, is very likely to *consist of* showing people what they are landed with – showing them, perhaps, that these enterprises are inevitable, or that certain features of life connected with them are inexpellable – even though the philosopher might also try to show them what it was (given these necessary features) to handle them reasonably or sanely or intelligently, perhaps in the light of what the enterprises were about or what their point was. For instance, we might be concerned with certain social or political affairs to do with authority and discipline and punishment; and the philosopher might want to show the conceptual inevitability of these concepts and practices in any human world (in case anyone thought he could evade or dispense with them), as well as saying something about what a reasonable authority, and a reasonable attitude to authority (discipline, punishment, etc.), would look like (Wilson, 1977). Or we might be concerned with the field of personal or emotional relationships: and the philosopher might want to argue for the absolute inevitability of (say) anger and guilt in human life (against anyone who dreamed that they were dispensable), as well as trying to consider what the reasonable man should be angry or guilty about (Wilson, 1971a; Strawson, 1962).

Philosophers seem to distinguish (generally speaking) only conceptual necessity from empirical possibility. Thus it would be a conceptual necessity that people (in the required sense) did things like choose, reflect, feel happy and so forth, since these are merely explications of what it is to be rational or conscious, but only an empirical possibility that they should (for instance) have hair on their heads. However, there are at least two other categories which need to be noted. Consider this passage from Quinton (1975, p. 19):

There are, indeed, other characteristics than rationality which seem to be common and peculiar to human beings . . . Examples would be laughing and cooking. But universal as these largely are among men they do not seem to be *essential* to humanity in the way that rationality is. It would, no doubt, be depressing to come upon a society of man-shaped creatures who neither laughed nor cooked, who met all changes of circumstance with straight or tear-stained faces and nourished themselves exclusively on the nuts and berries of folklore. But it would not inspire the thought that the creatures in question were not really men. After all there are unquestionably human beings here and there who, perhaps under the influence of Schopenhauer's philosophy or the macrobiotic ideology, neither laugh nor cook. Laughing and cooking, in other words, are factual not conceptual ingredients of human nature.

When Quinton says they are 'not conceptual ingredients' he must mean that they do not form part of the definition (the essence) of a man. For he sees clearly that there is *some* kind of conceptual connection, since his next words are

A further consideration is that laughing and cooking are, properly conceived, forms of rationality. To laugh is not just to go through a particular audible and visible physiological routine. The cachinnations of the hyena would be laughter only if they were the expression of an ability to see jokes . . . .

and so on. I think it could be shown, actually, if not that laughter and cooking (in their normal senses) were for conceptual reasons inevitable activities for men, at least that the ability to see and enjoy jokes, and the practice of improving one's food by some artificial means, were inevitable. But let us suppose that this is not so: we shall still not be correct in suggesting that laughing and cooking are merely contingent or (as it were) accidental facts, like the facts that most people have two legs and walk upright. There are two other possibilities:

(1) There is what we might call virtual conceptual necessity. A feature which is virtually necessary for conceptual reasons, in this sense, is one which it would not be contradictory to say is absent, but which will in fact almost certainly (still for conceptual reasons) be present. That is obscure: let me offer examples. Suppose we extend 'cooking', as we can do with other concepts, to 'improving one's intake of food or energy': taking it for granted, as it is fair to do, that any embodied creature in space-time must have some such intake. Then it is not impossible that the creature's foodstuff is and always remains perfect, in need of no improvement. (Actually this is extremely hard to imagine, which is why I take it to be a complete, not a virtual, necessity: but we waive that for now.) But, though it is not incoherent to say "The foodstuff always remains perfect", it is pretty clear that the chances are heavily in favour of something marring it at some time. This is simply to say that we cannot expect ideal circumstances to persist for ever. In much the same way, to take another example, it is not incoherent to suppose that a person never got jealous, because he never believed himself to have a right to anything other than his own; but in practice, since men are fallible, the chances are that he will. Similarly it could be argued (though, in my view, not conclusively) that a person might never do anything wrong, and hence never feel regret or remorse; but given a non-ideal world, it is virtually certain that he will. We rely here on a particular kind of input, the fact that the (any?) world is not ideal, and hence the features of the world are vulnerable: "time and chance happeneth to them all". I am not sure, and will not discuss here, whether this is best taken as a conceptual or empirical truth (I think the former); but in any case the truth itself, in conjunction

with other truths, yields what I have called virtual conceptual necessity – 'conceptual', because when the truth is added in we cannot coherently deny the virtual necessity.

(2) There is conceptual possibility; by this I mean that laughing and cooking, for instance, are not ruled out by the concept of a person taken with other concepts, indeed are as it were permanently on offer. People *could* always laugh and cook, as hyenas and jackasses could never. This is different from empirical possibility, and of course logically prior to it. If there is, for conceptual reasons, no (logical) chance of a person surviving physical death, for instance, then clearly there is no empirical chance either: conversely, if the concept of a person puts laughing and cooking on offer, we may then proceed to investigate whether the empirical facts (the existence of fire, for instance) make it possible.

If these possibilities for philosophy are real ones, can we say that philosophers – particularly modern philosophers, who deal overtly and self-consciously with concepts and conceptual argument – have taken them up and publicised them? Well, they have certainly been taken up: there is a great deal of work in both contemporary and past philosophy which is devoted to just this – indeed, in talking about this we are talking about the bulk of philosophical work generally. In other words, a vast amount of philosophical work does establish the kind of conceptual necessities and possibilities we have been discussing, whether or not the authors of that work saw it in that light. But it is, I think, in general true to say that it has not been seen in that light. Part of the reason for this lies in the self-denying and false doctrines discussed earlier (Chapters 1 and 2); but there is also some stiffer and more overt opposition. For various reasons not unconnected with a modern climate of relativism and excessive awareness of sociological fact, even very able philosophers deny or fight shy of this approach. One or two examples of this may be useful.

Toulmin at least faces the question squarely in his discussion of Kant and Strawson. I give one quotation at length:

In quasi-Kantian analytical philosophers such as Strawson, we find a further significant variation. Like Kant, Strawson

regards a certain set of basic terms and concepts as consti-
tutive of all coherent or intelligible speech and thought. Just
as the intelligible discussion of dynamics involves certain
inescapable theoretical concepts (e.g. 'mass' and 'inertia') so
one can talk or think intelligibly about anything whatever
only in terms of the corresponding everyday concepts: e.g.
'here' and 'there', 'before' and 'after', 'material object' and
'person'. But, in one respect, Strawson's view of this everyday conceptual framework is less grandiose than Kant's: the
basic framework of everyday concepts maps and delimits,
primarily, not so much the eternal, atemporal bounds of
coherent rationality as the actual, current bounds of intelligible sense. Instead of some mysteriously unique 'rational
coherence', what is now at issue is the more straightforward
and down-to-earth matter of sheer linguistic intelligibility.
And Strawson argues that human language, as we know it,
does rely for its intelligibility and effectiveness on its users
presupposing a sufficient common framework of basic everyday concepts.

About this Toulmin says:

Suppose that we ask Strawson the same questions as before,
about the implications of historical and cultural diversity; his
position leaves open one possibility which neither Kant nor
Piaget admits. If language as we know it relies for its intelligibility on its users presupposing a sufficient common
framework of basic everyday concepts, it is still open to us to
enquire: 'What if on some other planet, or in the remote
future or past, there existed communities of thinkers and
agents having their own shared conceptual frameworks – but
ones which did not overlap with ours enough to allow intelligible communication between them and us?' For anyone
who sets out to delimit the proper philosophical boundaries
of any rational thought or action, this hypothetical suppo-
sition is no more relevant than the actual facts of history and
anthropology. But a philosopher who claims only to be
demonstrating the bounds of sense cannot so well share
Kant's cavalier attitude to thinkers and agents in other
cultures or planets.

Later Toulmin adds:

> Strawson's final conclusions are, therefore, much more mod-
> est than those of Kant's position. The bounds of sense reflect
> the conditions of linguistic intelligibility, given human life
> and language as we know them. Conversely, given a non-
> human life and communication-system (or 'language') suf-
> ficiently unlike those we know, it becomes quite conceivable
> – even if only hypothetically, as a matter of science fiction –
> that there might be other, independent and non-overlapping
> 'realms of sense'. Within such an alternative realm, thinkers
> might understand each other perfectly well, even though our
> own attempts to make contact with them were all doomed to
> frustration. There would, accordingly, be nothing intrinsi-
> cally 'non-rational' about their thought and language; their
> modes of talking and thinking, reasoning and acting would
> merely be 'rational' in ways different from, and incommen-
> surable with, our own.   (Toulmin, 1972, pp. 425–7)

I am not here concerned with whether Toulmin here misrep-
resents Kant or Strawson (though I think he does), but rather
with the way in which philosophers allow themselves incoherent positions. Underlying Toulmin's difficulties is an idea of
language and even of concepts as changing, developing and in
general extremely sublunary entities. Thus "human language,
as we know it, does rely for its intelligibility and effectiveness
on its users presupposing a sufficient common framework of
basic everyday concepts" is tautological: it makes no sense to
say that there could be human language (as we *don't* know it?)
which did not rely on this. "There's a language but its users
don't have a common framework of concepts" does not appear
even remotely intelligible. The question "What if on some
other planet . . . there existed communities of thinkers and
agents . . . ?" is not really coherent: if such terms as 'thinker'
and 'agent' *mean* anything, then on this other planet there will
be thinkers and agents in *some* degree *like us*, i.e. possessing
whatever goes with the concepts marked by 'thinker' and
'agent' (e.g. being a person, doubt, decision, the will and a
whole host of others). The same applies, and here perhaps
most obviously, to " . . . it becomes quite conceivable . . .

that there might be other, independent and non-overlapping 'realms of sense' ". But 'conceivable' is just what it is not: for once we talk of rational life (even non-human life) and language and communication, we are immediately in a certain kind of business bounded and constituted by certain concepts. If Martians use a language in any serious sense, they must say things about things (subject and predicate), deny things (negation), and have a world of things and people to talk about (material objects and rational entities).

When it comes to practical enterprises, the same sort of things goes wrong. Toulmin (1972, p. 498) supposes it "impossible to lay down *a priori* standards of rationality for anything we shall acknowledge as (say) 'science' or 'law', in advance of any consideration of the actual diversity to be found in those enterprises": for "From what source do they derive their supposedly universal authority?" His own answer is "to refer neither to the timeless pursuit of abstract ideals, defined without reference to our changing grasp of men's actual needs and problems, nor to what the men of each separate milieu themselves happen to give the names of 'science' and 'law'. Rather, we work with certain broad, 'open-textured' and historically developing conceptions of what the scientific and judicial enterprises *are there to achieve*". That looks almost as if he thinks that there are, in fact, certain given goals or tasks (if not given *a priori*, then how?): but immediately there follows "These substantive conceptions are arrived at in the light of the empirical record, both about the goals which the men of different milieus have set themselves . . . and about the kinds of success they in fact achieved": we are to consider "how far . . . the alternative strategies employed in each milieu have actually fulfilled the historically developing purposes of the relevant enterprises". And now, either by 'success" he means something subjected to criteria which are not historical but timeless: or else to fulfil 'historically developing purposes' suggests a kind of survival-of-the-fittest view, whereby men in fact create the criteria of their own success. The former brings one straight back to Kant's attempt, the latter to some form of relativism: both he claims to avoid.

From the philosopher's, and also the educator's, viewpoint the empirical background – historical, sociological, psychological or whatever – is important ultimately only as enabling us to identify both the enemies and the allies of rationality. That is important enough: but it has no authority in point of reason, or rather it has authority only when philosophy has told us what proper reasoning is, what to count as a relevant fact and a good reason. Very often philosophy does this, not by abolishing whole swathes of discourse and activity but simply by clarifying them for what they are (astrology is harmless if properly understood: if properly understood, religion may be not only harmless but extremely important for the rational man). But unless philosophy could also rely on certain concepts, truths and criteria that were ultimately external to all sublunary enterprises – 'given' to us not by some notional authority to which we blindly defer, but because it makes no sense to deny them – neither Toulmin nor anyone else would know what to count as a 'relevant enterprise', let alone know what to count as 'success'. The enterprises we call 'science' and 'law' are relevant to embodied and conscious creatures, because part of the concept of such creatures is that certain goods (to control the physical world and a certain range of their dealings with each other) belong, as it were, to them. How clearly they perceive and pursue such goods is another (empirical) matter.

The second way in which philosophers have opposed this programme is less overt, and amounts in effect to a kind of heel-dragging; it is by the refusal to accept even fairly obvious conceptual connections, and a parallel insistence on treating what is conceptual as if it were empirical. A good, or at least a clear, example comes from part of a lecture of Warnock (1975, p. 35) in which he discusses "what, and how much, empirical information is required for, or relevant to, moral philosophy":

> For we are talking, of course, about practical principles: and that means at once that we should think of our rational beings not merely as rational (as 'pure intelligences') but as rational *agents*. But an agent, or at any rate a rational agent, has ends or purposes that he seeks to realise in action; and thus, though we are not yet anywhere near to insisting that our beings are human, we are taking them to be something

more than merely rational. Next, why does it *matter* what a rational agent does? Why does the question of right and wrong even arise? It is at any rate a large part of the answer to say: because he may have ends that it would actually be damaging to him to realise, or in seeking which he would frustrate realisation of the ends of others, or damage them. And thus we are supposing our beings to be not merely rational, nor merely rational agents, but in some degree *vulnerable* to harm at their own hands or at those of others; and we are supposing that ends are not necessarily all harmoniously co-attainable. But all this, though very general information, and indeed not information necessarily about humans, is *empirical* information; it does not follow from the bare concept of rational beings that they have these further characteristics or are placed in these circumstances.

A major difficulty, of course, is that the term 'rational' is (at this level of discourse) extremely obscure: partly, perhaps, because it is virtually a term of art in philosophy. But suppose, if this is not explaining *obscurum per obscurius*, that we are talking about an entity who (1) can think or reason, (2) is conscious of the world and capable of self-consciousness, and (3) is capable of considering alternatives. These (far too hastily-assembled) items are, no doubt, not discrete but connected both with each other and with other items – for instance, with the ability to use some kind of language: nevertheless, if 'rational' did not cover some such ground, one might reasonably be at a loss to know what the term meant.

Then it seems clear that such a creature (even if it could be coherently imagined as bodiless) will in some, perhaps fairly obvious, broad sense *do something*. It (he) will think, consider, contemplate: and it will have the option of reflecting on some things rather than others. Certain *preferences* will be inevitable: a preference for thinking about this rather than that, or for securing a state of affairs in which one thing is more readily available for contemplation than another, or for a state of affairs in which its powers of contemplation are maximised. Without *some* kind of end, desire, motive, or reason for deploying its rationality in one way rather than in another, that consciousness would be (as it were) unsupported: it would approximate, perhaps, to free association – but rationality implies more than that. Even the most disengaged entity – we may think of the depiction of alien beings as 'without emotion', 'coldly rational', or 'pure intelligence' – must have a reason for doing X rather than Y, or being in state P rather than in state Q (the alien beings commonly depicted by science-fiction writers are often motivated at least by curiosity).

Secondly, how could it not be at least *possible* that such an entity might damage himself and others? Rationality itself (let alone agency) implies the possibility of making *mistakes*, of things going wrong. Such a creature might omit to ensure its own survival, or the survival of others (sins of omission at least will be possible): and it will be vulnerable to other creatures in the same way. Whatever the creature does – even if its doing consists chiefly or wholly of contemplation – some set of circumstances is required as a precondition: and some item in that set might always fail, or be interfered with. It is not just, as Lucas (1966, p. 4) implies, that other creatures might inhibit its movements, as non-vulnerable tortoises might encircle one of their number: that is too narrow a concept of vulnerability. It is that (to use this example) the tortoise requires food, drink, light, a certain range of temperature, and so on. Some kind of controlled conditions (if not food, cosmic rays) necessarily pertains. Moreover – for it might, I suppose, be argued that in practice nothing need go wrong – some unknown external circumstance may always appear (invasion from outer space, a mutant virus, or whatever). Now it is always possible – and, we might argue, by the law of averages will at some time certainly happen – that one or more of these disruptive forces may fall into the hands or under the control of another entity: and, for similar reasons, that the other entity might not be permanently and wholly benevolent.

Arguments of this sort, anyway, must surely – whatever they may or may not prove in this case – be relevant. Above I have tried to show that there are (1) many real conceptual necessities connected with the notion of a rational being, and (2) many virtual conceptual necessities (as I have called them; see p. 62). This example is perhaps a little complex: but there are many simpler ones. (Consider, for instance, what is said by Hart and Lucas about their stipulations: see Lucas, 1966, pp. 1–5, with references.)

Does it *matter* (we might be inclined to object) whether we can prove the conceptual inevitability of certain features of human life? We might rather be tempted to adopt a fairly relaxed or down-to-earth attitude about this: we might say something along the lines of "Look, there is a department of life called 'sexuality' and 'sexual morality': now, the facts are that every human being is sexed, and every human society makes some kind of fuss about sex, so let's not waste time talking about whether the whole business is 'inalienable' for men – in practice it is there, and let's get on with trying to make sense of it and perform well in it." But that would be to miss the point in at least two ways. First, and very obviously, contingent changes (in technology, or biology, or some other field) might (and do) change the picture rapidly: and when the picture is thus changed we are left philosophically and practically unprepared, in a way in which we would not be totally unprepared if we had at least faced the question. Secondly, and more importantly, our answer to the questions "What is X?" and "What counts as doing X well?" will be very much conditioned by how we originally conceive of X. If X is, in however weak a sense, optional, then we shall be inclined to say certain things about it (for instance, to advance arguments about whether and when people *ought* to go in for X): if we see X as inalienable, we shall say other things. It ought, I think, to be tolerably clear even in advance that what we say, and how we argue, will be importantly different in each case. Thus it is important to know whether sex is an inexpellable feature of human life for every person, or just an option which a person might take up or not, like golf or fishing (Wilson, 1980).

It would not be too strong to say, then, that a too practical or down-to-earth attitude simply fails to face the question (let alone settle it). Moreover it is psychologically naive. Philosophers of this temperament are so anxious to be sensible and down-to-earth that, paradoxically, they allow ideology and fantasy to sneak in by the back door: for a Sartrean or Luciferian idea of human freedom will not only allow the possibility but demand the necessity of changing even the most basic empirical facts, or at least of regarding them as negotiable. Such ideas can only be satisfactorily quashed by showing that there are some (many) facts which it makes no sense to talk of changing, provided we wish to remain rational and conscious at all.

It is also easy to miss the extent to which the philosopher's arguments are undermined, or at least rendered harmlessly irrelevant, if we do not insist on what is inalienable to human life but rely simply upon linguistic facts. We may say indeed that *if* you have a word (say, 'triangle') with a certain meaning (including 'having three sides'), then there will be certain things you are forced to say, and certain things you cannot say, under pain of unintelligibility and self-contradiction. But this turns out to have severe limitations, since it says in effect only that words mean what they mean. Much of the criticism of linguistic philosophy has been to the effect that the meaning of words is a much trickier affair than might be thought. Sometimes we must look not for 'essential definitions' but for 'family resemblances': sometimes – or so it is said – we cannot pin the thing down in principle, since some concepts are 'contestable': and anyway (so the story goes) are not the meanings of words 'culture-bound', so that an analysis of them can tell us nothing of universal human interest? I hope to have shown that all these criticisms, except perhaps the last, are not to the point: at best, warnings of certain mistakes which we are likely to make *in* the task of analysis. But the question remains of how much this sort of philosophy is *worth* if it is based only on language.

One limitation seems inherent in the criterion of unintelligibility. Very elaborate arguments are produced by philosophers to show that – for instance – if we use the word 'ought' in its normal sense, or its primary sense, or at any rate in a certain described sense, then we are thereby committed (again, on pain of contradiction) to saying or not saying certain other things. But this is a big 'if': why should not someone simply say "Very well, I won't speak that particular language"? No doubt if a person goes in for a particular language there are reasons why he must or ought to speak it consistently; indeed that might be part of what was meant by 'going in for' speaking it. But what reasons are there why he should go in for it? Another limitation is at bottom much like the first, since it leads back to the same point: why should the particular use of language by, say, twentieth-century English-speakers be thought to be of more than sociological interest? If we are trying to establish important universal truths – and that might be independent of whether or not we want to go in for speaking a particular language – why pick English rather than Hopi Indian?

If one took that last question seriously, there might in fact be a lot to say about why it was more profitable to start with one natural language rather than another – apart, that is, from the (not unimportant) point that philosophers are more likely to be at home in their own natural languages rather than in foreign tongues. (Though this might cut two ways: one might be clearer about, say, classical Greek or Latin just because one does not take certain things for granted by speaking it every day.) But anything to be said along these lines would have to refer to some kind of external advantage: I mean, something which the philosopher hopes to achieve *by* getting clearer about what the words in a natural language mean. Now some philosophers, for all I know (it is difficult to be sure), might again take a fairly practical attitude about this: "The fact is that a lot of people do speak and think in English, or in languages sufficiently similar for the distinctions made in English to be reproduced in those languages: and getting clear about English meanings will save them from muddle and nonsense, and the havoc wrought by muddle and nonsense has very serious practical implications." But that is optimistic: people will be 'saved from muddle and nonsense' by clarifying their natural language only if they wish to continue speaking that language (or that part of it) and obey the rules that they now see more clearly. But why should they? Many in fact do not: rather than relinquish their inner feelings, fantasies and prejudices they are entirely willing to let the words run wild. It may now be said "Very well, but then why should anyone listen to them?" But they listen to themselves, and to anyone else whose words (no doubt equally wild) seem to echo their feelings. Then again it may be said: "Very well, but this is not a case for the philosopher: it is more a case for the psychiatrist"; but that is throwing in the towel too early, since we have not yet shown them why they *need* to speak that language properly.

What then should we hope to get out of conceptual arguments? I suppose something more or less Kantian, at least by way of conclusions (the nature or logical status of Kant's arguments, and what Kant thought their nature or status to be, are not clear to me). We want to be able to say "Men, indeed all rational creatures, are *landed with* certain enterprises, or ways of slicing up life, and also with other kinds of distinctions and concepts and features, in any possible world: so we had better face these facts, get clear about what the enterprises and distinctions are, and then get on with the job of analysing them more closely, in particular paying attention to what counts (in the light of the given nature of the enterprises) as doing them well." What would we mean, more precisely, by saying something of this kind, and how would we demonstrate it? There is one thing we certainly do not mean by saying, for instance, that men are 'landed with' these things: and that is, that men will inevitably *recognise* (and in consequence institutionalise – that is, put into practice) the distinctions. If that were so, there would be no need of philosophy to point them out; at best, philosophy could be seen as just sharpening up, or making more conscious, or articulating more clearly, concepts and distinctions that were already in some degree understood and institutionalised. Some people, indeed, talk as if they though that were all philosophy *did* do; but it is, pretty clearly, not in that direction that our hopes lie.

That, however, may be rather too hasty a way of putting it. For it is not usually a matter of just 'recognising' or 'not recognising': most cases lie somewhere in between. Suppose we consider a culture in which (as we, in our culture, might put it) no clear distinction was made between, say, art or 'the aesthetic' on the one hand and religion or politics on the other: thus, perhaps the inhabitants object (like the Chinese do or did) to Beethoven's music on the grounds that Beethoven was a 'bourgeois', or see paintings and statues not as pretty or ugly *per se* but, perhaps, as more or less theologically proper representations of the Deity (some Byzantines seem to have done this). Now do they recognise the distinction or not? Well, we might find (one is tempted to say, how could we not find?) that despite all this they still used, in everyday contexts, words meaning 'dainty', 'dumpy', 'pretty', 'nice to look at' and so on, without any apparent religious or political overtones: so that, in a way, or embryonically, or with some such qualification, we say that they do 'recognise' it. But they are not fully conscious of it, or perhaps they do not apply this aesthetic category to the objects to which we apply it.

In arguing with such people, as in arguing with (say) paranoiacs or certain kinds of religious believers, we appear to be doing no more than force a certain consistency upon them. Like Socrates we show the *incoherence* of their talk and their practices. Now it seems that this line of argument, or philosophical therapy, can only get going if *some* of the talk of the practice is already, as we would see it, sensible or sane. It is only if they do in fact use 'pretty', 'dainty', etc. round the dinner-table that we can enforce the distinction: only if the paranoiac sometimes uses, say, 'hostile' or 'plotting against me' in a normal sense (i.e. one which admits of falsification) that we can argue with him at all. Their 'normal usage' has not only to be normal in the sense of usual, but also (in our eyes) proper or coherent: it might not be usual at all – it might be that people spent much or most of their time in talking incoherently, at least in some areas (religion might be a good candidate here). Moreover it is clear that some groups might simply not mark certain distinctions at all. Determining such issues would be (partly) an empirical matter. Thus the general question, "Do men distinguish between (say) custom, law, etiquette, taboo, morality and religious injunctions?" is (partly) an empirical question: it is commonly said that, though twentieth-century English-speakers make these distinctions (as is clear, since otherwise we could not ask the question intelligibly), other groups do not and did not.

In effect this lands us with three different types of enquiry:

(1) First, there is the one just mentioned: the philosophically-informed but essentially empirical enquiry into whether, or to what extent and with what clarity, a particular group of speakers marks or marked certain particular distinctions (e.g. between custom, law, etiquette, etc.).

(2) Second, there is a philosophical enquiry into what distinctions or features *must* be marked by any language: that is, what is built into the notion of a language (for instance, the notions of subject and predicate, the law of non-contradiction, etc.).

(3) Third, there is a philosophical enquiry not about language but about the (rest of the) world, into what are the necessary features of any conceivable world with people in it (e.g. space, time, cause, embodiment, etc.).

The connections between (2) and (3) are important here. (3), being a philosophical enquiry, will be conducted both *in* and *by observing the logical implications of* language. That is, if we are trying to show (say) that anger is an inexpellable feature of human life, we shall both discuss this (here) in English and show that the concepts marked (in English) by 'man', 'desire', 'objective', 'obstacle', etc. entail the concept marked by 'anger'. But it will also be necessary to show that we are not just concerned with an oddity of English: that given certain concepts (marked in any way, not just by English words) with certain implications certain other conceptual implications follow. This is different from (2), because (2) is *about* language, in the same sense as that in which (3) is about the rest of the world (in my example, about man, space, anger, etc.). Nevertheless, the kind of argument we use for (2) is the same as for (3): we should try to show that a certain concept (marked for us by 'language') implies certain other concepts (predication, etc.). (2) is a sub-section of (3): language is *one* of the features of the world into which we may enquire.

The reader must not be misled by our talk of language into accepting two kinds of mistakes often made by students of linguistics (to use the common title of this discipline, whatever it may be). First, and worse, there is the idea that what are in fact inalienable features of human language can be (it is said, actually *are*) omitted by certain societies: second, a bit (but not much) less bad, the idea that if there are rival languages, conceptual schemes or sets of distinctions there is nothing to choose between them because there is no trans-cultural or extra-linguistic point on which we may take a stand. I will try to deal briefly with these.

(1) It is often said, for instance, that certain cultures 'have no idea (sense) of time': usually by linguists, who fail to find in some languages such precise terms as 'the day before yesterday', 'an hour and a half', and so on. But it is entirely clear that no conscious and rational creature could operate without the concepts of a past and a future, of events succeeding each other (this is bound up with another inexpellable set of concepts to do with cause and effect), and many other time-related concepts – for instance, memory, hope, fear, anticipation and so on. Of course just *how*, or how carefully, or for what particular purposes, or in what linguistic forms, they mark these concepts is another (empirical)

matter. But to say that they have no idea of time simply because certain *words* are absent is as absurd as to say that, for instance, the classical Greeks temporarily abandoned the idea of predication when they omitted the *esti* ('is') and just said *ho anēr kalos* ('the man is beautiful', 'is' being here understood) rather than *ho anēr esti kalos*.

(2) It is notorious that some cultures make more distinctions in certain areas than other cultures do – the Eskimos have lots of words for (different sorts of) snow, the Arabs for (different sorts of) camel, and so on. Some Indians are supposed to get by with only two colours – 'spring-leaf green' and 'deep blue' (though this seems wholly incredible: what do they do about the colour of blood, the sun, etc?) I have heard it argued that if that is their language, and if there were another language that had three (not just two) colours there would be no sense (point?) in asking which was 'right', or no way of adjudicating (perhaps even of making sense of) such a question, since what is or is not blue, green, etc. is entirely a function of the 'forms of life' and language that happen to be around. But this is plainly rubbish: we know colour-blind people are colour-*blind* because there are tests whereby we can prove that colours which they cannot see do in fact exist (they can be used to discriminate between otherwise identical objects, for instance). Apart from simple synonyms, no doubt Eskimo words for snow and Arabic words for camel indicate real differences between kinds of snow and camels, differences teachable even to brash Europeans who have not yet learned these distinctions or noted the differences on which they are based.

It is difficult, indeed, not to feel that linguistics as a subject (discipline, area of study); is an uneasy compound of two quite different elements: (1) a study of empirical and contingent facts about particular languages, and (2) a study of language in general, which ought to be largely a conceptual business. Thus if somebody were to claim or deny (as, in our own day, people like Skinner and Chomsky have at least seemed to claim or deny) that language-users must have some specific features in their brains or nervous system which enables them to learn a language, or that learning a language was in part a matter of experience and interaction with other human beings, or that no language could do without the concepts of subject and predicate, or anything of that kind, it seems quite clear that we are involved in some sort of conceptual or philosophical argument about what would or would not make sense to say – not, or not obviously, at least in the first place, a discussion of empirical facts. There may be empirical facts about language in general (that is, apart from actual or conceivable particular languages); but examples do not come readily to mind. I incline to suspect that linguistics has come to flourish so widely partly because of a climate in which conceptual truth has been misunderstood, and in which people prefer some kind of ideology to the study of particular facts about particular languages. However, some of this may be unfair and unkind: I raise the points simply to reiterate the conceptual–empirical distinction in another context.

I have accepted the point that conceptual arguments, to be effective in empirical practice, have to start by assuming some kind of empirical input. The input I have assumed is the existence of people; and it is worth noting that this does not grant much space to any critic who might wish (a) to question whether this assumption can yield very much, or (b) to question the assumption itself and (hence) the value of any conceptual arguments that can get going on its basis. For (a) I have suggested that the concept of a person – though I shall not argue further for this here – may be thought to involve a whole host of other notions: it is not, in my judgement, a coherent idea that there could be people existing without some kind of bodies, or outside space and time, or without such things as thoughts, intentions, plans, goals, motives (emotions), choices between the more or less desirable, and plenty of other things – some of which are themselves conceptually connected (most obviously, the idea of embodiment with the idea of space). Then (b), what in fact is it to 'question the assumption' of there being people? Certainly, it makes sense to *say* "There might not be any people"; and we might easily imagine everyone on this planet (and any other inhabited) being destroyed. It also makes sense to ask and argue about whether one ought to resign from being a person, by (say) committing suicide, or with the aid of some drug or brain operation reducing oneself to the animal or vegetable level. But what makes the idea of questioning the existence of people in some *general* way seem unreal is, surely, more than just the (admittedly coherent) possibility of these contingencies: it is that all discussion or argument about what there is or what is to be valued – even discussion about the contingencies themselves – takes it as given that there are existing people who are engaged in such discussion. If that is an 'assumption', it is so only in a rather curious sense. We do not exactly 'assume' that there are now people with whom we are discussing these matters: their existence is part of the discussion.

Two more points need to be made here. First, it seems generally true to say that philosophers have been more successful in meeting the demand for certain knowledge about the world than in meeting demands about how to live or conduct practical enterprises. That may be partly because the most able philosophers of the modern age (with many notable exceptions) have preferred to concentrate on the former rather than on the latter: they have seen – and, again, an argument can be made in favour of this view – work in areas commonly put under the headings of logic, ontology and epistemology as central and work on ethics, politics and human nature as peripheral or even as derivative (although of course, they are connected via the philosophy of mind). But an additional reason may be that in these latter areas, more closely concerned as they are with human nature and values, philosophers are more liable to prejudice, fantasy and blindness arising from their own individual natures or even from the influence of their society or social position – this latter point, of course, being one which sociologists and others who revel in the variety of human social life indefatigably and triumphantly insist on (see e.g. Macintyre, 1966). It is not so much, or not only, that one may echo or react against particular values; it is also that one may take certain prevailing category-types or enterprises for granted, thus overlooking the possibility both of new categorisations and of changing the priorities in existing ones. For example, it is (to say the least) not clear that the vast amount of work put under the heading of 'morality ' is properly so placed – particularly since we have no very clear and agreed delimitation of that category. Still more importantly, comparatively little work has been done on aspects of human nature which may be crucial – for instance, on love and the emotions generally, the unconscious mind, and a whole swathe of issues which have been tacitly handed over to developmental and clinical psychologists or even to literature, just as many of the issues in political and social theory have been (rather more obviously) handed over to sociologists and ideologists. That may be at least one of the reasons why progress in this general area seems to have been so slow. Unfortunately it creates the not unreasonable impression that philosophers can only produce proofs on matters where no serious person really has any doubt, as for instance about the existence of the external world or of other minds: whereas when it comes to human nature and how to live, they have little or nothing to tell us.

We may hope, then, for much more work within this second area – that is, where conceptual truths may be elicited that have to do with human nature, values, and society. But – and this is my second point – any truth there may be in the view just expressed, that philosophers have not made as much of that area as they might have done, should be a ground for only cautious optimism. It is fatally easy to think, or hope, that one can prove by conceptual argument a vast quantity of truths that one would very much like to see proved: the immortality of the soul, the durability of love, the greater permanence and reality of the general as against the particular (or vice versa), even the existence of some kind of god – briefly, many of the things that men have sought in religion or in philosophies of life for lack of finding them in philosophy proper. That holds too for practical enterprises: the philosophy of education, to take a particularly striking example, has consisted almost entirely of philosophers (even very good philosophers, like Plato and Russell) simply *using* the idea of education as a peg on which to hang their own particular ideological values. We desperately need solid ground here.

All this may still sound rather too general, even vague: so I should like in the next chapter to offer two brief examples of the kind of task I have been describing, so that the reader may be left in no doubt about what that kind is. The examples come from my own work: partly for convenience, though chiefly because I try in them not only to show certain conceptual necessities, but also to show (1) how even competent philosophers can have blind spots about such necessities, and (2) how the understanding of these necessities makes a severely practical difference to our thinking. It needs to be added, of course, that there are a good many examples (though not as many as there should be) in more authoritative writers (Strawson's *Freedom and Resentment* (1962) is a model case in recent times). For my own examples I hope only that they are clear, brief, and illustrate my main thesis adequately even for the philosophically untrained reader.

4 Two Examples

(A) PUNISHMENT AND AUTHORITY

A set of interconnected concepts – 'authority', 'rules', 'punish-ment', 'institutions', and others – mark, as I see it, logically inevitable or inexpellable features of human social life or interaction: concepts which are bound to have some appli-cation or instantiation, and which it will be both senseless and unnecessary to 'challenge', 'question', or 'justify' in general. This view stands in fairly sharp contrast to a good deal of philosophical literature; and the contrast is particularly evident in relation to one of these notions, the notion of punishment. For fairly obvious reasons, this notion has caused a good deal of soul searching among the tender-minded, and forms a good point of entry. Thus Peters, in a section entitled 'The justifi-cation of punishment' (1966, p. 169):

> Punishment, then is retributive by definition. It is part of the meaning of the term that it must involve pain or unpleasant-ness and that it must be as a consequence of an offence. . . . It is not a law of nature that if people commit offences pain is inflicted on them. This happens regularly only because men have instituted legal systems which ordain that offenders will have pain inflicted on them. People brought up under such systems therefore tend to make this retributive relationship hold. But the question has to be faced by rational men whether it is appropriate both that pain should be inflicted when a rule is broken and that it should necessarily be inflicted on and only on the person who has broken the rule. How can these normative demands built into the concept of 'punishment' be justified? . . . The answer given to this question will depend, of course, on the general ethical theory which a man adopts.

Similarly Hirst and Peters (1970, p. 128):

> 'Punishment' in its central cases, has at least three logical necessary conditions. . . .
>
> i. It must involve the intentional infliction of pain or of some kind of unpleasantness.
> ii. This must be inflicted on an offender as a consequence of a breach of rules.
> iii. It must be inflicted by someone in authority. . . . This introduces the question of the justification of punishment.

In general, a utilitarian line is taken, according to which 'Punishment is a necessary mischief, the lesser of two evils' (ibid., p. 129).

This picture has certain internal oddities and obscurities. Thus it is odd to make pain a central notion here; comparatively few punishments involve pain. Even 'unpleasantness' seems not strictly necessary – how far they enjoy it or like it does not seem to be central; the point is rather that this is something enforced on them whether they like it or not. Again, 'as a consequence of' hardly makes us clearer; if I beat a boy who has broken a rule, and we want to know whether this is meant (or taken) as punishment or shock treatment, nothing is gained by saying that it is done 'as a consequence of', 'because of', or 'for' the breach of rule. The sense of 'for' which we need is actually very hard to elucidate: it is certainly nearer to 'in return for' than 'as a consequence of'. (Try paraphrasing 'for' in 'three for a shilling', 'I'll get you for this', 'he paid for it', 'the French for "dog" ', 'a medal for bravery', etc. 'Retribution' does not make anything much clearer.) These oddities are, I think, symptomatic of a picture of punishment as a contingent and prima facie highly objectionable phenomenon. Now contrast the following argument:

(1) Anything that could seriously be called a 'society' or 'social group', as against a collection of hermits who happen to be living in the same area, involves some kind of interaction between its members; and 'interaction' here will not mean just that they bump against each other like

physical objects, but that they engage in some rule-following activity – even if, as perhaps in the case of a seminar or a tea-party, the activity consists only or chiefly of linguistic communication. There will therefore be rules or norms which are commonly subscribed to, whether or not they are codified, overly agreed and stated before-hand, or contracted for.

(2) A breach of these rules must, at least characteristically if not in every case, be taken to entail the enforcement of some disadvantage on the breaker. If this were not so, we should not be able to identify them as rules prohibiting X and enjoining Y, rather than enjoining X and prohibiting Y; or else we should not be able to identify them as rules at all, as against wishes, pious hopes, generalisations about human behaviour, or descriptions of some sort of ideal. A social rule enjoining X exists only if, when people fail to perform X, something which is characteristically a disadvantage is normally enforced on them.

(3) Various words may be in place for the type of disadvantage – 'punishment', 'penalty', 'sanctions' etc. – as well as for the form of disadvantage – 'ostracism', 'imprison-ment', 'exile'. Not all these disadvantages will be painful (going to prison does not involve pain), but they will all be characteristically 'bad things', otherwise they would not be disadvantages but rewards. Thus loss of liberty is, characteristically, a 'bad thing'; though a man may some-times, even often, find a situation where he is told what to do is more pleasant than a situation where he can do what he wants, he must in general wish to retain the option of liberty so long as he continues to see himself as a human agent. (This is why 'unpleasant' is not quite right.) Fur-ther, whether or not the group gives some of its members particular authority to interpret and enforce the rules and disadvantages, the disadvantages will in every case occur by reason or in virtue of the rules that constitute and govern the group's interaction. That the group subscribes to these rules, or that the rules are in force, logically entails disadvantages to rule-breakers, whether or not these disadvantages are properly called 'punishments' inflicted by special authorities.

(4) In English we speak of 'punishment' in reference to the

common and criminal law, and in reference to some institutions with limited sovereignty (for example, schools). With games, and (perhaps) generally in cases where we wish to avoid the implication of moral blame, we prefer to speak of 'penalties': elsewhere we may talk of 'sanctions' or more vaguely of 'being made to suffer for' a breach of rules (for example, of social etiquette). Other languages may not make these distinctions, which may indeed sometimes seem arbitrary: *poena* in Latin, for instance, covers a wider range than our 'punishment'. The question thus arises of whether we are trying to 'justify punishment' in reference to the particular (and, it may be thought, in some degree arbitrary) range of instances for which we use the word 'punishment' (and not 'penalty', 'sanctions' etc.), or whether we are to 'justify' some more general concept.

(5) If some more general concept is at stake, it is presumably the concept of being (as I have called it) 'disadvantaged' in virtue in rules governing social interaction. But we have seen that such disadvantaging is logically entailed by the notion of social interaction. What could it mean to 'justify punishment (disadvantaging)'? I suppose some such question as "Why should we have any form of social interaction and rules at all?" might be coherently raised (though I doubt this) but it would be necessary to raise such a question in order to make any sense of 'justifying punishment' as a whole. More probably a person who, in real life, protests against or demands justification for punishment objects to one or other of the *kinds* of punishments, or rules, or authorities, or systems in force: but this is a different story. He may also be led to raise questions about the whole conceptual apparatus of which punishment is a part – the whole 'basis of authority', as it might be called; and some of these questions, as we shall see below, are both intelligible and important. But that too is a different story.

(6) If, on the other hand, we are interested solely in the specific concept of punishment as the word is used by English-speakers, it will be difficult to know how to proceed. For suppose that we dismantled the legal system of judges, codified laws, specified penalties and so on; then

plainly there would still remain most or at least some of the forms of social interaction, with rules and ensuing disadvantages, even if these disadvantages were not formally administered in courts of law. The same criteria as those commonly listed by philosophers for 'punishment' would pertain: disadvantages would still be given by the social group for breaches of the rules. Whether or not we would continue to call these 'punishments' rather than 'penalties', 'sanctions', etc., seems to me an open question, and not a very interesting one. Certainly they might be just as harsh, or perhaps harsher; laws and school rules may be severe, but the sanctions or penalties imposed by mobs, bullies and even the peer group may well be more so. Arguments for or against the specific form of sanctions which seems to be implied by 'punishment' – perhaps a comparatively high degree of formalisation, or codification – would be heavily dependent on empirical facts; off-hand one might be inclined to suppose that the degree of institutionalisation implied would improve clarity at least, and hence (other things being equal) be a more desirable form than more unpredictable, because more informal, methods. But however that may be, we are now clearly involved in a discussion of the best *kinds* of sanctions or disadvantages; not what is commonly taken as 'the justification of punishment'.

What seems to have gone wrong is this. Philosophers of a utilitarian turn of mind have seized on 'the infliction of pain' as something prima facie morally objectionable. Forgetting the conceptual connections we have outlined above, they have then asked 'whether it is appropriate . . . that pain should be inflicted', suggested that 'the answer given to this question will depend on the general ethical theory which a man adopts' and talked about 'the refusal to attach sanctions to socially important rules', as if this were an intelligible empirical possibility. But it is not. (Cf. Strawson, 1962; Hart (quoted in Peters 1966, p. 285) says "That is how human nature in society actually is, and as yet we have no power to alter it." 'As yet' makes no sense in my view (nor I think, in Strawson's).)

This perhaps brings a little nearer to the surface a common contemporary attitude which we find in many teachers and educators and social workers already, and which philosophers ought to be curing rather than reinforcing. It is as if Kant's community of angels were regarded as a conceptually coherent ideal. The attitude emerges in such passages as (Peters, 1966, p. 279):

> The truth of the matter is that punishment in a school is at best a necessary nuisance. It is necessary as a deterrent, but its positive educational value is dubious. Education cannot go on unless minimum conditions of order obtain, and punishment may on occasions be necessary in order to ensure such conditions. . . . Under normal conditions [*sic*] enthusiasm for the enterprise, combined with imaginative techniques of presentation and efficient class management, will avert the need for punishment.

In the parallel passage in Hirst and Peters (1970, p. 129), 'under normal conditions' is well replaced by 'ideally'. If one has a concept of punishment which is divorced from the more general idea of sanctions and penalties, and which is tied fairly tight to the notion of pain, then of course this makes a kind of sense. But what we have to remember is that, in so far as there are clear and operative norms or rules, then precisely to that extent failure and breaches will be penalised in some way.

Indeed this seems to be more than just a social matter. In so far as I, even alone on a desert island, seriously propose to myself ends or goals and rules for achieving them, to that extent I shall necessarily blame myself when I fail through my own fault: I shall feel remorse or regret, guilt or shame – we might even talk, more or less metaphorically, of my 'punishing myself'. This goes together with 'enthusiasm for the enterprise', not against it or as an alternative strategy to it. Success and failure, and hence in a broad sense 'rewards' and 'punishments', are inexpellable from human life. An individual or society may, of course, change the norms (just as, in the way we saw in (6) above, the types of sanctions may be changed); and one way of doing this precisely is to take away their sanctions, which at once *eo ipso* removes their status as norms. For instance, if being a nuisance in school or society characteristically results in a person's receiving more attention and care (support from counsellors and welfare services, and so on) rather than some disadvantage, then there is no longer an operative norm or rule – though there may be one on paper – against 'being a nuisance'. The norm has in effect become just a pious hope. This sort of situation does, I think, pertain in many schools today; and perhaps also, to no inconsiderable degree, in society at large. It is as if we were no longer sure what actions we wished to bring under the whole mechanism of justice: and this may have the effect of making us lose our grip generally on the concept of justice itself and its attendant concepts, of which punishment is one.

For much the same reason two other notions (among many), generally marked by the terms 'authority' and 'institution' are also inexpellable. Any society or interacting group of rational creatures must have a common decision procedure: indeed this can be taken as a defining characteristic of a society (Lucas, 1966, pp. 10ff.). As Peters (1966, p. 238) says, the notion of authority "presupposes some sort of normative order". But it is also presupposed by it; and it is not true, as he says in the same context, that "We can conceive of a society of highly moral beings living together amicably out of respect for a moral law and for each other as rational beings, without anyone being in authority, and without anyone being thought of as an authority." The reason is not only because men are inherently non-angelic, 'bloody-minded' as Lucas calls it (p. 1), but because in order to express their amicable disposition and 'have respect . . . for each other' such beings would need decision-procedures and authorities to operate them. If you cash out the notion of 'normative order' into actual cases of things that these beings might do – exchange goods, play cricket, hold debates, run railways, or whatever – the point becomes clear. Authorities (referees, arbitrators, umpires, etc.) are necessary, not just to punish vice, but to provide clarity in those rule-governed activities; 'the editor's decision is final', not or not only because somebody has to mark down incompetent entries, but because it has to be clear what counts as winning the competition. In the same sort of way (the argument need not be put on stage again) the structural contexts which incorporate and clothe these activities – that is, 'institutions' – are also inevitable (Wilson, 1977, pp. 48–53).

(B)   FORMS OF KNOWLEDGE

Philosophers – particularly philosophers of education with an interest in questions about the curriculum – have a strong interest in classifying different kinds or knowledge. I shall consider here one classification which is very well known: the following quotations from its author (Hirst) will be enough to start us off:

(a)   In the developed forms of knowledge the following related distinguishing features can be seen:

    (1)   They each involve certain central concepts that are peculiar in character to the form. For example, those of gravity, acceleration, hydrogen, and photosynthesis characteristic of the sciences; number, integral and matrix in mathematics; God, sin and predestination in religion, ought, good and wrong in moral knowledge.

    (2)   In a given form of knowledge these and other concepts that denote, if perhaps in a very complex way, certain aspects of experience, form a network of possible relationships in which experiences can be understood. As a result the form has a distinctive logical structure . . . .

    (3)   The form, by virtue of its peculiar terms and logic, has expressions or statements (possibly answering a distinctive type of question) that in some way or other, however indirect it may be, are testable against experience. This is the case in scientific knowledge, moral knowledge, and in the arts, though in the arts no questions are explicit and the criteria for the tests are only partially expressible in words . . . .

    (4)   The forms have developed particular techniques and skills for exploring experience and testing their distinctive expressions. (Hirst in Dearden *et al.*, 1972, pp. 405ff.

Elsewhere the same author distinguishes seven forms: logic/mathematics, physical science, interpersonal knowledge, moral knowledge, aesthetics, religion and philosophy. He adds:

(b) The differentiation of these seven areas is based on the claim that in the last analysis, all our concepts seem to belong to one of a number of distinct, if related, categories which philosophical analysis is concerned to clarify. These categories are marked out in each case by certain fundamental, ultimate or categoreal concepts of a most general kind which other concepts in the category pre-suppose . . . . It is these categoreal concepts that provide the form of experience in the different modes. Our understanding of the physical world, for instance, involves such categoreal concepts as those of 'space', 'time' and 'cause'.

Concepts such as those of 'acid', 'electron' and 'velocity' all presuppose these categoreal notions. In the religious domain, the concept of 'God' or 'the transcendent' is presumably categoreal whereas the concept of 'prayer' operates at a lower level. In the moral area the term 'ought' labels a concept of categoreal status, as the term 'intention' would seem to do in our understanding of persons. The distinctive type of objective test that is necessary to each domain is clearly linked with the meaning of these categoreal terms . . . .

The division of modes of experience and knowledge suggested here is thus a fundamental categoreal division, based on the range of such irreducible categories which we at present seem to have. That other domains might, in due course, come to be distinguished, is in no sense being prejudged; for the history of human consciousness would seem to be one of progressive differentiation. (Hirst and Peters, 1970, pp. 64–5).

We are bound to raise the question of what this list of forms is a list of. Now the answer we might expect is something like this: "Look, all over the world people have to make decisions about what to teach children. Obviously it will be useful for them to have a sort of logical guide-book to what kinds of knowledge there can be. Some of these areas that we've demarcated – morals, religion, aesthetics – may be a bit obscure; but there's surely a case for saying that there just are, from a logical point of view, these different kinds of knowledge. What we're offering is a timeless, culture-free sketch of the logically different kinds of things that rational creatures can know, or the logically different modes of knowledge that are possible." In other words, we would expect this to be a strictly philosophical enterprise along traditional lines.

In fact this is not a correct interpretation, as appears from the final remarks of Hirst quoted in (b) above: 'categories which we at present seem to have . . . other domains might, in due course, come to be distinguished'. The general intention is echoed by Dearden (1968, pp. 64–5): "What actual forms of understanding men have evolved . . . can be determined only by an examination of the knowledge that we do now have, and not in any high-handed a priori way." But now we have a worry which can be represented as follows:

(1)   If the concern is with what 'men have evolved' or 'we at present seem to have', then who are 'men' or 'we'? Pygmies? Witch-doctors? Astrologers? Are 'we' the avant-garde of 'human consciousness', or just typical representatives of it, or what? In so far as this is an empirical thesis about what 'men' have done, it ought to be made much clearer what 'men' we are talking of. Some 'men' (social groups) do not distinguish or differentiate as 'we' do – for instance, they do not count morality and religion as separate domains; and the 'we' who have 'evolved' the highly monopolistic concept of religion ('God', 'the transcendent', 'predestination', etc.), or the particular utilitarian-style version of morality ('respect for persons', etc.), may not be either typical or, necessarily, more sophisticated or 'progressive' in our 'differentiation'.

(2)   If now we want to say that 'we' are the avant-garde, that people ought to differentiate because in some sense there just are those distinctions (whether or not people actually make them), then this (sociological) interpretation becomes incoherent. For on what basis could it be said that the distinctions are there, other than on some strictly

logical basis which is not intended as culture-bound or time-bound? We can of course investigate, *qua* philosophers and not just *qua* sociologists, distinctions which are drawn and recognised, albeit vaguely, by 'us'. But either we face the question of whether these are 'real' (i.e. logically sound or necessary) distinctions, or we do not face it. If we do not face it, then this is just a rather sophisticated sociological thesis – and certainly we should have no valid reason for recommending these distinctions for curricular purposes. If we do face it, then we must have some culture-free criterion for determining whether the distinctions are 'real' or not; and this criterion must presumably be found somewhere in the realm of logic or conceptual necessity.

It might be thought that this is to wield too sharp an axe. Consider a parallel with animal taxonomy. Some societies may not distinguish mammals, vertebrates, reptiles, etc., as zoologists do, preferring perhaps other distinctions (edible and inedible, easy or hard to trap). Nevertheless we can say (1) that there really are these zoological distinctions, and (2) that we are still not operating 'in any high-handed *a priori* way'. We are not precluded from saying that there may be other kinds of animals which we have not yet discovered, or new kinds that may arise, which would add to our taxonomic list; yet we might also feel able to claim that our taxonomy was in some ways more profound than one based on such distinctions as edible – inedible – that ours did more justice, so to speak, to the real nature of the animals.

That is the best I can do for this interpretation of the forms of thought; but it is still not quite good enough. One consideration is that taxonomies have to be judged on their purposes. There would be no point in the distinctions of zoology if they did not help us to make sense of certain problems and phenomena – the evolutionary history of animal species, for instance. If we can understand evolution, or the distribution of species in the world, or something of that kind, only by the use of these distinctions, then (only) are we justified in claiming that the distinctions are important irrespective of whether particular social groups made them – we would now say, recognised them – or not. For then they are underpinned by culture-free considerations. In the same way, the forms-of-thought taxonomy must ultimately be justified by whether the logic of different forms really is different, not by whether 'we' or any other social group actually make these distinctions. To repeat: if 'we' *qua* philosophers are trying to produce a list each item on which is *sui generis*, then 'we' cannot ultimately rest content with the 'differentiations' which 'we' currently make *qua* members of certain twentieth-century cultures. 'We' (*qua* philosophers) have ultimately either to endorse these differentiations or reject them.

This does not mean that there is anything wrong with using the 'categories which we at present seem to have' or 'the knowledge that we do now have' as a basis; that is, as data – even perhaps as a prima-facie taxonomy – to be philosophised about. Nor, equally, is it necessarily false that 'other domains might, in due course, come to be distinguished': but this will have to mean, not just that some social group may come to make new differentiations (rightly or wrongly), but that the distinctions are logically sound – and this means, in effect, that more progress will have been made in logic (in a broad sense) or philosophy. To use our parallel; it is not so much that new species of animals may be discovered on Mars, for instance, and that we cannot do anything about categorising these until time passes; it is rather that, by very hard thinking about the animals we already have available, we may be able to notice new distinctions.

Whether or not these considerations would be acceptable to Hirst and others, it seems clear that they are relevant to the obvious deficiencies in the more suspect forms (morality, aesthetics, religion). In this light, we should surely not adopt a programme of waiting to see whether, for instance, various societies severed religion from morals, or regarded literacy, musical and artistic criticism as different genres (as we now to some degree regard biology, chemistry and physics as different). For we should still have to say whether these moves were proper or improper. And this involves wrestling with the enterprises or 'forms of life', which have thrown up such subject-titles as 'religion': what we have to take seriously is not the titles but the genres. There is no short cut to this.

Of course the process is extremely difficult. But it is not made easier, more down-to-earth, or less 'high-handed' by

representing the programme as just a matter of observing the
'progressive differentiation' of 'human thought'. For we immediately run into well-known difficulties which recent philosophical debates have brought out. For instance: one author
says of a particular magical or superstitious belief of the
Azande that:

> The Azande do not intend their belief either as a piece of
> science or as a piece of non-science. They do not possess
> these categories. It is only post eventum, in the light of later
> and more sophisticated understanding, that their belief and
> concepts can be classified and evaluated at all.   (Macintyre,
> 1964, p. 121)

Now one might well doubt whether there could be any society
in which, as the author says, there was a *total* 'absence of any
practice of science and technology in which criteria of effectiveness, ineffectiveness and kindred notions had been built up':
rather as one might doubt whether there could be any society
without a norm of truth-telling, or any language without subjects and predicates. But one's doubts here are logical and (if
you like) *a priori*, not sociological doubts. We might end up,
with the Azande and other cases, by saying something like
"Well, in a way they differentiate and in a way they don't", or
"They don't differentiate as clearly (consciously) as we do." In
other words, it is not just a matter of seeing whether the
Azande have 'science' on their school time-tables; it is a matter
of classifying 'in the light of later and more sophisticated
understanding' – and to do this, we have to be sure that our
understanding *is* more sophisticated (that is, more philosophically and timelessly correct) rather than just 'later' or different.

From this point of view we may not only find the categorisation of the suspect forms (morality, religion, aesthetics) in
Hirst to be over-hasty: we may well think the categorisation of
the first two or three to be over-modestly presented. Whatever
distinctions may be valid here – for instance, some sort of
distinction between analytic and synthetic knowledge, or between our understanding of persons and our understanding of
physical objects – they are surely not just valid for our language or our society or our planet. If somebody said that there
were or could be Martians who did not make some use of these

distinctions and who operated without such concepts as 'space' and 'time', 'person', 'intention', and the like, I think we should be unable to understand him. His picture would be as incoherent as that of monsters from outer space whom science-fiction writers try to represent as 'rational' but totally without 'feeling' or 'emotion'. Arguably also there are conceptual reasons why some mode of moral thinking, some kind of aesthetic experience, and perhaps even some religious activity are inevitable for rational creatures: or at least (we might for some purposes want to add) for creatures that develop from children into adults, rather than springing fully-armed and equipped into immediate maturity. This possibility is what makes the task of delineating these forms or modes worth a philosopher's while to attempt; whereas (to put the point extremely) a more sociological progamme might conclude that 'aesthetic experience' was merely a curious cultural phenomenon originating in Bloomsbury in the 1920s.

Hirst's more recent remarks do not, in my judgement, make his position any clearer. On the one hand he says

> As distinct from a Kantian approach, it is not my view that in elucidating the fundamental categories of our understanding we reach an unchanging structure that is implicit, indeed a priori, in all rational thought in all times and places. That there exist any elements in thought that can be known to be immune to change, making transcendental demands on us, I do not accept. (Hirst, 1974, p. 76).

Even in its context, this is very hard to understand. If someone said that notions like subject and predicate, truth and error, non-contradiction and many others were not 'immune to change', I think we should be at a loss to know what he meant by such a phrase. The notion of a logical or transcendental demand has sense just because we recognise paradigm cases of it, which we contrast with what is changeable. To put this another way: for something to count as 'an element in thought', it would have to satisfy certain criteria: there are analytic truths and logical entailments which set the rules for what we can intelligibly think and say. If someone were to claim, for instance, that there could be coherent or rational thought that paid no attention whatsover to the law of non-contradiction, we should not understand him. If this were not so, philosophy and logic would be indistinguishable from sociology and empirical linguistics.

A further passage reads:

> Nothing can any more be supposed fixed eternally. Yet none of this means that we cannot discern certain necessary features of intelligibility and reason *as we have them* . . . we can pick out those concepts and principles which are necessary and fundamental to anything we could *at present* call understanding. . . . Intelligibility is itself a development in this context, and one that is of its nature hedged in and limited by it. To assume that this framework is in any sense necessarily fixed now seems absurd. But to imagine it is not setting limits to what is *right now* intelligible is equally absurd. [my italics] (ibid.)

But the trouble here is the same as before; the ideas fall half-way between sociology and logic, between the empirical and the conceptual. 'Intelligibility' and 'reason' are normally taken to mark transcendental notions: that is, either something is intelligible (reasonable) or it is not. Certainly we may come to see that something is or is not intelligible, by the usual processes of philosophical clarification; and certainly we may start to speak a different language, whereby (the rules being changed) collections of signs that were intelligible become incoherent, and vice versa. But that is all that could be meant by the italicised phrases ('at present', 'right now', etc.).

There are, surely, some considerations which would make it worth our while construing our procedure along lines opposite to those taken (perversely, as I see it) by Hirst. We need not specify these lines in advance by terms such as '*a priori*' or 'transcendental': but we have to show, by conceptual rather than empirical argument, that certain basic types of experience giving rise to certain structures of thought and language are inevitable for any rational creatures living in a space–time continuum. In fact, our difficulties here are due mostly to the fact that philosophers have paid remarkably little attention to those experiences and structures which (to put it briefly) have more to do with emotion than with perception; hence it is quite unsurprising that our specific doubts about Hirst's forms of knowledge increase, as we saw earlier, the further we remove ourselves from logic and science.

We can, without too much difficulty, see what sort of conceptual arguments make it inconceivable for such a creature to have absolutely no kind of logical, scientific, or personal knowledge. To advance much beyond this would involve constructing a conceptual network based on the (given) fact that the creature has desires and emotions as well as intelligence, and the logical inevitability that these desires and emotions will be characterised by what might be called a common case-history. It seems reasonable to doubt whether we could proceed very far without paying rather more serious attention to the unconscious mind than philosophers have hitherto been accustomed to do; and it is certainly on the cards that existing titles – 'morals', 'personal relationships', 'art', 'games', 'humour', 'religion', 'politics', 'ideals', 'ideologies', etc. – will need a good deal of revision (Wilson, 1979a, pp. 110–18).

The importance of appreciating such conceptual necessities ought to speak for itself; but I should like to add a word or two by way of conclusion, since the ideas involved are very much out of keeping with the modern intellectual climate. We can see, at any rate, that they give philosophy a good deal more weight than just that of a tool and incentive to internal coherence and consistency. The broad outlines of what the world is like and how we should handle it are not up for grabs, but given. Philosophy demonstrates the skeleton, as it were, of the world and man's place in it, leaving other disciplines to fill in the fleshly details. As that metaphor suggests, there is no question of the details being unimportant, or even (whatever this might mean) less important than the skeletal outlines: the point is rather that the details must depend on the outline, as the flesh hangs on the bones – and this means that, generally speaking, there is a certain temporal (as well as logical) priority to be given to philosophy. We must know the limits and parameters within which we are working: in particular, and perhaps most obviously, the *shape* of a practical enterprise (education, politics, etc.) before we can have any clear idea whether our detailed moves are sensible or not.

This is of course an extremely old and orthodox view,

exemplified in the work of many philosophers, but (as I see it) stated in its most persuasive and psychologically perceptive form by Plato. (Much of this book, as many readers will be well aware, might be read as a modernised and more boring version of parts of the *Republic*.) I share also with Plato the view that philosophical *education* is critically important, the reason for this being ultimately that without such education any changes that occur in the social or individual consciousness, though they might be accidentally for the better, are at best unreliable and insecure. No serious progress in, for example, such enterprises as politics or morality or religion or mental health or personal relationships (though Plato did not think much of these latter) can be expected unless we are sufficiently educated in dialectic or philosophy to appreciate the relevant Forms or concepts. Without that we live in the cave, and take shadows for reality. This is not a popular modern idea (particularly in education), and I will illustrate by example. Suppose we wish to avoid racial prejudice and its ill effects: then it might be said, with some prima-facie plausibility, that to try and do this by philosophical education – by discussing the concept of a person, the relevance or irrelevance of race or colour, etc. – would be, at the very least, unnecessarily time-wasting and circuitous. We should get results more quickly, cheaply and securely by some non-rational process, such as subliminal advertising, or brain-washing, or a propaganda campaign: or if, as is currently the case, there is a sort of liberal prejudice against such dramatic methods, then we should create a climate of opinion, a wave of fashion against which few people will want to swim (which is, in fact, barely if at all more 'rational' a method than the other, though it creates more of an illusion of free choice). Perhaps, as a sort of intermediary move, we hire a beautiful black girl or stalwart black boxer to appear on television to convey the message that black is beautiful and strong and in general a good thing.

The first thing to notice here is that this is not and could not be a case of rival methods to the same end: certain ends logically go along with certain methods. The use of what we have called 'non-rational methods' – propaganda and so forth – cannot produce greater rationality (that is why we call them 'non-rational'). Hiring beautiful blacks may change the prejudice so that people are now in favour of blacks rather than against them: and that may, politically and in other ways, be a good thing. But it cannot in itself teach, explain, demonstrate, or (in general) promote *understanding* in people (though it may lay the groundwork or create conditions for the promotion of understanding): for that, we have to use such processes as explanation, discussion, argument, the deployment of evidence, and so on. If our end is to lessen *prejudice*, to increase rationality in this area, then we have to use these methods: if our end is some 'brute' phenomenon, such as the absence of certain behaviour (riots against blacks or whatever), then other methods can do the job.

But why (it may be asked) is this an argument for philosophy, rather than some other rational discipline? Indeed, could not someone be reasonable (unprejudiced) about race without any kind of rational thought at all? Might he not just be secure or loving enough to have escaped the common prejudices? Or if he requires education at all, might not some historical thought – the history of the slave trade, for instance – do just as well as or indeed better than philosophy? Much turns here on just what we want. We might be content with people who, for a period of time or in certain contexts, were reasonable about race: or who, so far as their lives had gone hitherto, had felt no temptation to be unreasonable: or who had been powerfully moved by some historical facts or perhaps a vivid film (and now we might be worried by the nearness of this method to the advertising campaign mentioned earlier) to adopt a pro-black attitude. For certain practical purposes we may be right to be content with such. But all of them are, as is clear enough, *fragile* in their allegiance to what is reasonable (if indeed they have any real allegiance at all) about racial matters: it cannot be otherwise, because their views and attitudes, though they may coincide with those of a thoroughly reasonable person, are not securely founded. The only secure foundation must include a proper understanding of why, in fact, it actually *is* reasonable to think such-and-such and not to think so-and-so; and this is, in large part, a philosophical matter – that is, the reasons require some philosophical grasp of the relevant concepts. For example, someone who thinks that it is just in some way wrong – illiberal or unkind or something – to use "Because he's black", without further explanation, as a reason for denying a person food or clothing or education has not gone far enough: he needs to see that such a reason *makes no sense*, that it is not even a respectable candidate for a reason. Otherwise he is likely to see himself as representing some (mutable and fragile) ideology, placed in combat against other ideologies and, ultimately, with no more right to be heard than they.

Further, by being able to appreciate the real reasons in such a case the man will be able to generalise more effectively and over a wider area. By grasping the relevance or irrelevance of (say) colour, he comes to grasp the same points about race, creed, sex and so forth: he does not limit his rationality to treating blacks as equals, but extends it to all people, since he sees that (cutting a long story short) it is their being *people* that counts, and not these other things. If we tried to fulfil ends as broad as these by non-rational methods, we should find it difficult or impossible: an advertising campaign for or against blacks, or women, or some other particular and visible class is comparatively easy, but how do we advertise rationality or irrationality, relevance or irrelevance? The fact that abstract and general principles are involved is precisely what constitutes the strength of philosophical change: it makes the individual both ultimately *secure* in his rational beliefs (since he is not just wedded to them *ad hoc* or for a time, but rests them on the ultimately valid reasons for them), and makes the beliefs sufficiently *potent* (for, being general rather than specific to a particular context, they have wide application).

One might ask, as Plato did, whether (in view of the difficulties) it was necessary that all or even most or many people should be changed in this way: could not the élite be trained philosophically, and the rest of us just do as we were told? To some extent, we may be forced by practical limitations (such as the stupidity or bloody-mindedness or mental illness of certain people) to adopt this policy; but the reasons for lamenting such limitations are clear enough. First, we need a wider base to approve and sustain such an élite: the élite may not last long unless a lot of ordinary people understand enough about philosophy to see its importance and to vote for philosophical rulers. Second, there are many things in life (and those not the least important) which we have to do for ourselves, and where it makes no sense to talk of others (the rulers) doing them for us by command. I may effectively obey a command to kiss my wife, look at a picture, listen to Mozart, and repeat the words "I forgive my enemies", but I cannot *just* by virtue of obedience to orders (though orders may help) love and understand my wife, appreciate the picture, enjoy Mozart, or actually forgive my enemies. These things require a fuller understanding and co-operation on my part. Thirdly, even in those cases where ends can be achieved simply by obedience, there can be advantage in added understanding: as children, though they can and often have to obey in ignorance, may do so more effectively if they understand something of the reasons behind the orders.

Even here we have to beware of slipping into a doctrinaire and currently fashionable 'democratic' position; and arguments are available to counterbalance the three points made above. First, it may be inevitable or more efficient to concentrate on the philosophical training of a particular élite, if only to generate a wider base of public support (thus Hare (1971, p. 39) believes that the 'Oxford tutor' by teaching those who will 'reach the highest ranks of their professions . . . can have much more influence on the life of the country'). Secondly, given a wide enough sense to the phrase 'under orders', much more may be done by placing people under orders than might be supposed: pupils, for instance, are under orders in this sense when they are compulsory placed in contexts which effectively educate their emotions and make them better able to love, forgive and appreciate – the strictly logical point that one can only do these things for oneself does not support any generally 'liberal' or 'progressive' educational régime. Thirdly, there are many contexts (and not only military ones) in which the effectiveness of autonomous thinking is outweighed by the possibilities of such thinking being irrelevant or misguided.

It is, clearly enough, an open and (for the most part) an empirical question who ought to be philosophically trained and how, the answer to which will depend on many variables: the general strucure of a society, the temperament of the person being trained, and so forth. But we certainly cannot assume that any Platonic pre-philosophical programme (e.g. *Republic*, 521ff.) will be a practical possibility in any society as it now actually exists; nor, indeed, that such a programme will obviate all the difficulties that people have in learning philosophy: these difficulties lie very deep, and it is not to be believed that a firm grounding in mathematics or other disciplines will turn out ideal students who will take to philosophy as ducks to water. Either the problems will appear at the earlier stage of prephilosophical training or, more probably, they will show themselves as soon as they face up to the demands of philosophy. Hence, on any account, it will be very important for any serious philosopher to understand these problems and difficulties in philosophical education. This will be our concern in the next chapter.

5 Reactions to Philosophy

This chapter-heading is the best I can think of to include a somewhat heterogeneous set of topics, all of which nevertheless seem not only relevant to 'what philosophy can do' but also connected with each other. For unless we confine the word 'can' to a severely restricted sense, what philosophy can do depends very much on certain practical considerations – how it is conceived and received in the practical world, what sort of opposition or alternatives to it we may expect, what philosophers need to bear in mind when teaching it, and so on. These topics, though in a fairly clear sense practical, are notwithstanding closely connected with the nature of philosophy (on which I hope to have shed at least some light in previous chapters): hence these are not matters that can be turned over too blithely to sociologists and psychologists and other empirical workers, though it would be highly desirable that philosophically-informed empirical workers should tackle them (as, to date, they have not).

Some may still think this range of topics, sufficiently great to be daunting in itself, to be also irrelevant to what philosophy can do; as if there were a clear distinction between the nature of the subject and its presentation, or between content and style. From an empirical (and particularly a pedagogic or educational) viewpoint that is, of course, naive: and arguably it is naive from a logical viewpoint also. In practice, philosophy is an attempt to marry our beliefs and feelings to the real world by means of exact descriptions and conceptual clarity: and in so far as that is true, justice has to be done to both partners in the marriage – that is, to our (incohate or autistic) beliefs and feelings as well as to the impersonal standards of conceptual truth. The feelings and beliefs have to be taken seriously.

That is more obviously true when we consider the teaching of philosophy: no student is likely to learn much (of any permanent value) about certain topics – perhaps notoriously in the area of moral and political philosophy, though not exclusively there – unless his own feelings and views, however primitive, are taken account of. To demand their total suppression is in its own way as misguided as to endorse them in their primitive form (for instance, by presenting him with a ready-made ideology which does no more than institutionalise the feelings). But it must also be true, though the phenomenon may be more masked, that the professional philosopher is fighting the same battle, even if at a more sophisticated level. It is not (as it is sometimes represented) that moral philosophers, for instance, first have strong feelings about morality and then leave these feelings behind in their philosophising: nor only that they may be driven to philosophise because of these feelings: but rather that these feelings accompany them, in some form or another, and of course not necessarily at a high temperature, *in* their philosophical work.

It is notoriously difficult (and might even be thought impossible) to keep feelings alive and free from distortion without the ability, on some occasions to express them spontaneously and in a sufficiently unsophisticated form. The proper balance between spontaneity and deliberation, a very general topic of great importance, cannot be discussed here: but it is at least clear that there may be excessive weighting or misuse on either side. Unsurprisingly, philosophers present at least the appearance of having come down too heavily on the latter. Into whatever reality may lie behind this appearance it would be impertinent to enquire too deeply, and anyway impossible to enquire with much hope of success; nevertheless it has to be said that philosophers, at least, do not present a very welcoming aspect. Even allowing for the undue deference, nervousness or sheer paranoia that may afflict the layman when he thinks of approaching professional philosophers, and remembering of course that popularity and accessibility are not the only nor perhaps the most important features of a good educator, we have also to remember that for most purposes and most of the time, the outsider has to deal with an image or self-presentation. On that understanding, it is (I think) fair to say that many philosophers present themselves as essentially *remote*. (Thus it has been said of Ryle – by any reasonable criterion one of the kindest and most helpful of men – that he *edited* his feelings and self-presentation, and thus for some people (arguably, no doubt, the naive) appeared remote and impersonal.)

Some may see here a parallel with the non-directive psycho-therapist, who also edits his personal reactions and emotions (briefly, in order not to play the patient's game) and inevitably conveys something like the same impression of remoteness. But the parallel soon breaks down. The psychotherapist's attitude is artificial and deliberate, and (in a successful course of treatment) is progressively shed: further the patient comes with particular problems and particular kinds of motivation. A philosopher might perhaps defend a similarly remote self-presentation on similar lines: but that defence would have to rely on (amongst other things) the assumption that professional philosophers should only swing into action when their patients (or students, or interlocutors) were already in a state of highly-motivated doubt or *aporia* — that is, had already reached the stage of trying to marry their feelings with reality and were passionately desirous of help given by a benevolent and skilful neutral. That is perhaps an attractive idea, but a very puristic one: if philosophers should not always be Socratic gadflies, they cannot always be consultant conceptual physicians either.

Comments on the personality, if not the character, of philosophers in general may indeed be seen as impertinent in the usual sense of that word: but these topics are not impertinent in its root-meaning of irrelevant. There are important and intellectually demanding questions here for all who teach philosophy (or even write it, since that is a form of teaching or communication albeit at long range). Just what sort of image should one present – or, if that sounds too much like an advertising campaign, just how should one behave towards one's pupils? How does one make the subject seem attractive and interesting without playing to the gallery, or demonstrate the kind of enthusiasm that must be displayed in any effective pedagogy, towards both the learners and the subject (most of us are biased in respect of one or the other of this pair), without becoming facile and fulsome? How, in particular, is one to improve oneself when one has recognised one's deficiencies – is it any good trying to work at it by sheer will-power and practice, or is some more serious attempt at self-understanding required?

These are not rhetorical questions, but clearly they cannot be answered here. I raise them chiefly because it is easy for us not to take them seriously: we hide a certain laziness in trying to answer them and act on the answers beneath talk about integrity and sincerity and an exaggerated dislike of the inflated or the phoney. But there are more ways than one of being autistic: and any of us that does not, within reasonable limits, do his best to face them betrays not only pedagogy but philosophy. For not many of us (I hope) will want to say that philosophy is merely a hobby, or justify our pursuit of it by reference to purely selfish reasons: it *matters*, and if it matters then it cannot matter only to us – it matters to those other people whom we instruct and converse with, so that we have a double duty not only to say what is true and helpful but to say it in a helpful and effective way.

On any but the most naive account, teacher–pupil relationships in philosophy are of very great importance: greater, at any rate, than in those subjects which are less 'personal' both in the sense that they characteristically have less effect on the pupil's inner life (that is, if he gets seriously engaged), and in the sense that there is less room for idiosyncratic responses. With many other subjects, much of the teaching can be as well or better done impersonally, by mass lectures or text-books: the pupil has merely to grasp the facts. In such a position, which it is not at all absurd to liken to the psychoanalytic transference, two opposite temptations occur. Some are tempted to make their teaching too personal, or personal in the wrong way, forgetting about the principles and procedures of the subject, and perhaps liable to use their pupils in order to gratify their own desires: others may be so keen to avoid this that they forget about the person altogether, and may even be blind to the fact that effective learning in this area, as in many others, inevitably depends on a proper handling of the personal relationship.

Whilst generalisation is rash, I have little hesitation in guessing that many philosophers succumb more to the second than to the first temptation. This may have something to do with a dislike of the facile, the pretentious, the phoney, the muddled, and the superficial which is certainly a prerequisite of any serious philosophy. Thus Jean Austin, in an otherwise admirable article on teaching moral philosophy (Austin, 1973), lays great stress on the opposed notions of integrity, honesty and veracity, and she disclaims

> . . . the least intention on my part to approach the subject or the teaching of it in a personal way, in the sense in which one would aim at probing into the personalities of one's pupils or trying at all to indoctrinate them or, from my point of view, 'worse', guide their private lives. There are few things I should be more reluctant to do.   (p. 27)

Something has gone badly wrong here, because philosophy plainly does require a 'personal' approach in some sense of that word, and would not be worth much if it did not (however indirectly) guide a pupil's private life. The author is creditably hesitant about illegitimate imposition or indoctrination: but these notions are not properly opposed to impersonality. The approach and effect of Socrates' teaching forms a fairly sharp contrast with this apparent puritanism. I stress this because in practice young people will be guided, treated 'personally' and psychologically engaged either by proper philosophers like Mrs Austin, or else by ideologists and other gang-leaders. Teachers of philosophy require a notion of integrity which makes allowance for this fact.

Be that as it may: teaching philosophy is an extremely difficult, as it is an extremely important, task. The only way to make any progress is to try to understand the reactions which people have to philosophy itself, and to reason in general. These reactions have to be understood both by the layman and by the professional philosophers: there might then be some hope of improved communication, where we now have a kind of hit-and-miss system in which most laymen (not only students) feel extremely uncertain about the whole business. In the rest of this chapter I shall be trying to say something helpful on these (admittedly very broad) topics.

The social position of professional philosophy need not, I think, detain us here very long: it forms the sharpest possible contrast with our claims for it – claims which remind us more of the traditional picture of philosophers than the picture of the philosopher as a highly specialised and isolated professional. It is towards the former picture, certainly, that I would wish the reader to turn his attention; for it is, in a sense, a political or historical accident that philosophy has become isolated in this way. The internal causes of philosophy's becoming specialised – roughly, because of an intense though quite proper preoccupation with methodology (Ryle, 1956, pp. 2ff) – coincided, in most western societies, with an increased democratisation and egalitarianism which brought a diminished respect for any experts who had not (as scientific experts had) proved their worth to the general public. Over the last fifty years, very obviously in the UK, though perhaps less so in other countries where non-ideological forms of philosophy have flourished (the USA and the Commonwealth), an atmosphere has been created or strengthened in which the idea of moral or political experts, let alone Plato's philosopher-kings, no longer seems even faintly plausible. Any connections there ever were between the social order and philosophy, or even between the social order and the general idea of wisdom as represented by academics in philosophy or cognate disciplines, are now tenuous to the point of non-existence.

In so far as any discipline now generates sages, they may be put roughly under the headings of sociology and psychology. As I have tried to show, some of the blame for this must be laid at the philosophers' door, both for a too timid attitude towards their own discipline and for exceptionally bad public relations. But, of course, as I shall try to explain, there are sharper resistances to philosophy than to these other enterprises; perhaps things were bound to go that way, whatever philosophers did. But the resulting situation is in two fairly distinct ways alarming. First, philosophical considerations are virtually excluded from government: and this is alarming for anyone who, like Plato, thinks that good government is impossible without proper understanding of the relevant necessary truths about human life. (Even those who think that philosophy can only contribute negatively or therapeutically must be alarmed, since there is little evidence that it does actually make this contribution: one looks in vain for signs of it among politicians, trades-union leaders and other figures of influence.) Secondly, philosophy is also pretty well excluded from various individual enterprises where it is needed: not only from the enterprise of politics itself (where the rules, limiting concepts, and characteristic virtues and vices are exceptionally badly understood), but also from (a) theoretical enquiries like sociology and psychology, the methodology and presuppositions of which are chaotic, and (b) practical enterprises such as education and the mental health industry, of which the same is true.

That is a depressing picture, but not (I think) an unjust one. The question arises of what can be done to improve things. Any answer will in large part turn on where one thinks is the best place to break into what is clearly a vicious circle: individual fantasy generates or permit institutions and political systems which in turn generate or tolerate fantasy in individuals. In one way we may seem worse off than Plato, inasmuch as there is no single individual or single small body of individuals – no Dionysius of Syracuse – whose conversion to philosophy would in its turn convert the citizens of a whole state (not that Plato, I take it, was ever quite so naive as to believe this to be a serious possibility); but philosophical understanding, in any case, cannot (logically cannot) be imposed – it is something each individual has to learn. We have at least free communication and expression, and an educational system in which we invest heavily: but then again, it is not clear that the pressures of fashion and the values of the market-place which democracy allows are any less compulsive, though they might be less brutal, than those more overtly wielded by totalitarian societies.

That, if still sounding pessimistic, may make for realism: only slow and patient progress is to be expected. Yet we can do a little better than such truisms as that. We can get clearer about that vital area in which men have both freedom and real opportunities for change: that is, the area in which a process of philosophical and psychological awareness both of the conditions of life and of our own natures may, though with difficulty, enable us to think and act less like puppets. As I shall try to show, philosophy is powerless unless combined with the education of our emotions, in particular of our unconscious emotions; we may also remember that no such education, and no serious psychotherapy beyond the level of purely physical methods (however desirable such methods may be in a particular cases), can be coherent and effective without proper philosophical understanding.

Hence we need not, I think, waste any more time in considering the attitude of the state or of society or of people collectively: that is a function of philosophy's failure to make itself understood and valued by enough (or enough important) individuals, partly because (leaving aside its intrinsic difficulties) since early in this century it has become highly professionalised and specialised (Ryle, 1956, p. 3). No doubt other social, political or institutional pressures also apply – the demand for what is 'relevant' or 'practical' in higher education, for instance. But, as this point shows, there must lie a lack of understanding at the bottom of this: philosophy *is* (in the required senses) 'relevant' and 'practical', it is just misunderstood. Nor is it only misunderstood, as if mere ignorance were the chief reaction. That is far from the case. People find it difficult (alarming, objectionable) in a quite different way to that in which they find, say, *The Times* crossword difficult. They *react* against philosophy.

What is the nature of these reactions? Of course people may well have certain standard reactions towards *any* subject, or discipline, or expertise with which they are not familiar: it is hard to distinguish these from reactions to philosophy as such. Secondly, of course different people react in different ways, so that generalisation is dangerous: a difficulty compounded by one's uncertainty about whether a reaction is caused by a person's individual psychology (if I may so put it) rather than by his vested interests as the occupier of a particular role or doer of a particular job – whether, so to speak, he is reacting as a person or as a role-filler. Thirdly, there is a worry about whether one can classify reactions to philosophy in anything like an exhaustive manner: whether one may be omitting whole categories of reaction which one has never come across or simply forgotten about.

But, perhaps with undue optimism, I do not take these difficulties as overwhelming: I am bold enough to believe, after a good deal of experience and consultation with other philosophers, that these reactions are fairly specific to philosophy, fairly limited in number, and above all fairly easy to identify – in brief, that they are very *obvious* reactions, often so predictable as to be boring. Much more serious is the difficulty of categorisation if one makes any attempt to explain them. It is hard to describe reactions without one's description overlapping into some kind of explanation (indeed the distinction is a hard one to make even in theory): and the problem then arises

of what level of explanation to attempt. For the various remarks, images, emotions and other constituents of the reaction
do not, of course, exist in self-contained boxes: they connect
with deeper features of the human mind. But with this difficulty I can do no more than compromise: I attempt here only a
list of the most common reactions, together with some ex-
planatory remarks which could no doubt be pressed much
further (by a clinical psychologist, for instance). Perhaps others
will be able to improve on what I say: certainly I hope they will,
since the subject seems of very great importance.

Part of that importance derives from the fact, as I take it to
be, that philosophy is in a unique position. I used to believe
that this was because what philosophers did was uniquely
mysterious to the layman. There may indeed be something in
this idea: it is tolerably clear to laymen, or at least intelligent
laymen, what *sort* of thing historians or physicists or archaeol-
ogists are doing, what their fields are *about*, even if the actual
work is a closed or unintelligible book. But there is more
bafflement, or a different kind of bafflement, about what
philosophers think they are doing, and why they are doing it,
and why they think it important. (We all know why nuclear
physics is important, however little we understand it.) But I
now incline to the view that the mystery is not to be properly
located in the content or methods of philosophy – which,
indeed, can be explained fairly easily in principle to any intelligent person, even if the explanation has little force without
supporting example and detail. I think it has more to do with
the style and image of some philosophical talk.

If the layman were presented merely with the unknown and
(in a sense) the arcane, with a discipline that had its own jargon
and its own mysteries which were visibly mysterious, he would
find it easier to handle: and in one way laymen were in fact
more comfortable with philosophy when it was practised in this
arcane, high-minded way, even though (or perhaps because) it
deployed a language of its own – the Absolute, the Good Life,
and so on. Nowadays he is presented with philosophers who
appear to talk English, usually quite ordinary down-to-earth
English: only – and this is what makes it baffling – he cannot at
all see what they are talking *about* or even what they are
talking *for*. They are not – or so they say – trying to sell a line
about what Reality is like, or what the Good Life consists of:

they do not take sides, which would make it easier to join in. Nor – or so, again, they say – are they just interested in linguistic tidiness, pedants of language who may at one time be dismissed as over-fussy and at another found moderately useful when we need to be particularly precise. Nor, for most of the time, do they seem concerned with giving neutral accounts of what previous philosophers have said, which would again be moderately intelligible (a course on Great Thinkers of the Past).

I can think of only one parallel, and that by no means exact. Characteristically the layman will find what competent psycho-therapists do baffling in much the same way (even when he is undergoing psychotherapy), and make analogous moves. Surely the therapist must have certain moral values or attitudes which he is trying to sell to the patient, surely he must be indoctrinating or conditioning in some way. Or if not that, surely he must have some arcane theory of the mind, just as the physicist has theories about matter: he must be armed with all sorts of concepts and technical terms that the layman has not mastered. Or if not that, perhaps he is just a kindly person with plenty of common sense, a good friend, who has somehow managed to get paid for listening to people with problems. Of course (as with the case of philosophy) there is *something* in all these reactions. Competent psychotherapists have some con-cept of sanity, know some things about the mind which laymen do not know, and should possess both kindness and common sense. But none of these quite captures just what psycho-therapists actually do or why they do it.

Nearly all, perhaps all, the reactions to philosophy are attempts to turn it into some more easily recognised or stereo-typed activity. Perhaps these can in fact be listed fairly briefly, though each category contains many variations.

(A) IDEOLOGIES AND -ISMS

Since many people called philosophers in the past (and some, I regret to say, even today) do in fact take some kind of ideologi-cal stance or count themselves as adherents of a particular school or -ism, the laymen may be pardoned for assimilating philosophy to this stereotype. The philosopher must, it is believed, whatever his actual talk or professed purposes, be a Marxist, or a humanist, of the left or of the right, a believer in this or that set of 'values', possessed even of a particular *political* (certainly of a moral) stance. Even if he is not actively engaged in selling this, he must – in a useful contemporary American phrase – be 'coming from there': there must, surely, somehow, be a set of assumptions, some kind of metaphysic or world-view, on which he relies as a basis for what he says. The truth, which is (briefly) that philosophers should make no such assumptions but rely solely upon the notions of conceptual or logical coherence or incoherence, is remarkably hard to believe: particularly when philosophers stop doing philosophy and start selling ideologies, thus justifying the stereotype.

A slightly different version of this reaction is found amongst those who have heard something of the history of philosophy, and are thus able to avoid facing philosophical issues by classifying what is said as representative of a particular school or -ism. This is, so to speak, an academic rather than an ideological classification: the speaker will be tabbed as a Platonist or an Aristotelian, a 'utilitarian' (whatever that is) or, to quote an example still commonly found, a 'logical positivist'. This classification serves a double purpose: it suggests that the philosopher can be disregarded (because there are rival 'schools', and who is to say that his is the right one?), and it also relegates him to the world of theory or academia, thereby defusing or castrating the practical relevance of what he says – as in (B) below.

(B) 'THEORY'

Since some philosophers seem very enthusiastic about what they say, and since some seem to be very clever, but since also what they say seems to have no relevance to the world as the layman knows it, it is plausible for him to believe that the philosopher must dwell in some other world: a world of 'theory', or an ideal world, an ivory tower in which he contemplates and argues about things as they might be (not as they might in practice be made to be, but as they might be in some Utopia) rather than about things as they are. They are idealists, starry-eyed, their heads in the clouds: the rest of us have to live in the world as it is, and can merely disregard them.

There are two versions of this reaction also. The more modest, or at least more polite, escapist regards it as all right for the philosopher to inhabit this world: he may even think it is desirable to have some people around who are more high-minded or idealistic than the rest of us – it adds tone, or culture, or respectability. In the same sort of way people want there to be saints, even though they do not seriously think they ought to follow their example. The less inhibited escapist regards the philosopher as dangerous, since he may mislead practical people by his Utopian talk; or at best as wasting time and money, since he does nothing useful.

(C) 'JUST ABOUT WORDS'

Laymen who have cottoned on to the fact that philosophers are interested in words and the meanings of words may still be baffled about why they have this interest, or what the interest is. It may seem (i) as if they are interested in words for their own sake, perhaps as grammarians and philologists are; or (ii) that they are just more fussy about verbal precision than the rest of us; or (iii) that they are particularly concerned with definitions, fallacies, ambiguities and other such. None of these are, of course, entirely wide of the mark; but none appreciates the relationship (no doubt disputable) between words, things and reality which gives philosophy its point.

When something of that relationship is appreciated, it may seem (iv) as if the philosopher does in fact have an assumption – perhaps in a sense an ideological assumption and hence properly to be classified under (A) above: briefly, the assumption that 'ordinary English' or 'normal usage' has some kind of authoritative status. The philosopher is taken to believe that the way in which 'ordinary English' marks out the world – a way which naturally connects with the interests and values and prejudices of English-speakers – is somehow *the* (right or proper or best) way. Either – so it seems – it just happens to be the case that English works in the way it does, which may be of interest to linguists and others but gives us no right to use it as a basis for saying anything important; or else the tacit claim must be being made that English enshrines reality in some uniquely desirable or authoritative way – and why should anyone believe that? The same dichotomy might be applied to 'concepts', about which philosophers talk freely: why should concepts marked in twentieth-century English be of more than linguistic or sociological interest? This (very common) reaction justifies, I hope, the attention we have paid to these matters in earlier chapters.

It is worth adding to these a few reactions which occur specifically when, as sometimes if all too rarely happens, the layman decides to 'bring philosophy into' some kind of enterprise. It is almost always occurs when there is some kind of pressure from outside, or from some extremely vague notion of academic respectability: thus educationalists and those in charge of social work, to take two examples out of a severely limited stock, are apt on occasion to believe that philosophy must somehow be 'relevant'. The reactions here all take the form of avoiding the only task worth pursuing, which is actually to *do* some philosophy *in the context of* the enterprise itself (rather than separating it off into some adjacent compartment).

We can mention these quite briefly. There is (1) the addition of courses not properly or at all integrated with the enterprise: thus those responsible for training social workers may add a course on ethics because ethics seems 'relevant', but the ethics *of social work* is (often) not discussed at all. There is no hard philosophical interchange between moral philosophers and those who lay down guidelines for social workers, for instance: the cutting edge is taken off philosophy by relegating it to a course on the sidelines. Similarly in (2), the use of 'authorities' in philosophy, brought in often just for the sake of respectability. I remember one set of lecturers responsible for educating some (fairly simple-minded) teachers of science, who made them read philosophical authors whom even those fairly experienced in philosophy might well find hard to grapple with (Habermas and Kuhn, in this case). Unfamiliar with philosophy, the lecturers either did not appreciate that this was a bit like making students who could hardly add grapple with the binomial theorem, or students quite unfamiliar with Greek palaeography attempt to decipher the Linear B documents. But the proper alternative of actually raising and discussing philosophical questions relevant to teachers of science (and there are plenty of such questions) would have involved both lecturers and students taking philosophy seriously and actually *doing* some, rather than just wrapping up some respectable-looking philosophical packages. What might count as a different and still more disreputable reaction, (3) the occasional pietistic references to Wittgenstein, or Russell, or some other well-known philosophical 'name', is still widely indulged in: the idea being, I suppose, to display breadth of scholarship and wide reading. But about this horror we need say no more.

Slightly more interesting in principle, if intensely boring in practice, is the reaction (4) of doing something which resembles or at least caricatures philosophy *in sociologese*. Because of the almost total disconnection between philosophy and the social sciences, sociologists and others have found themselves desirous to express points of methodology or procedure, often conceptual points, but without the philosophical training and experience necessary to do so clearly and economically. Long-winded and very obscure passages, indeed whole articles and sometimes even books, studded with the ritual references to other (sociological) authors and suggesting the amassing of evidence for some empirical thesis, or discussions of various 'research paradigms', 'social methodologies' and so forth, are often to be construed as attempts to make some – often fairly simple – conceptual points, usually in the philosophy of mind; and some of the writing in social science connected with rationality and relativism is best read as primitive attempts, as it were by a first-year student who has not yet got the hang of what philosophy is but has an interest in the appropriate problems, on well-known topics in ethics and epistemology. (Of course there are honourable exceptions to this.)

I have spoken of all these reactions as arising from a kind of bafflement, and as if they came in to fill the space (as it were) which an understanding of philosophy alone could fill properly: as if philosophy had to be misinterpreted or misconstrued by means of models more readily intelligible because more familiar. This seems to be true so far as it goes, but it does not go far enough. For why, after all, should the layman simply not remain baffled, without forcing what he does not understand into some mould which he does understand, at least until he begins to get some idea of what philosophy really is?

There seem to be three possible lines of thought here. One is the well-known idea that the human mind, like nature, abhors a vacuum: that men feel a very strong pressure to classify and categorise. That is certainly true, and (given certain inevitable parameters about the development of a rational mind) may even be a conceptual truth: how, after all, could a man make sense of the world without such pressure? At the same time, however, we do assimilate new cases and even invent new categories, though admittedly with some difficulty: and there are, after all, some actual philosophers in existence, who must have picked philosophy up from somewhere. A second idea, also fairly obvious and well-documented (Plato has a great deal to say about it), is that the stereotypes to which philosophy is falsely assimilated are not just inert categories, but have compulsive force of their own. This is perhaps most plausible in the case of our first reaction, which involves the stereotype of ideology: we might say that people feel so strongly about their own ideologies, and are so used to advancing or defending them, that philosophy is (for them) inevitably drawn into this magnetic field. But this seems a bit less plausible for the other reactions; though it might, no doubt, be argued that the relegation of philosophy to the realm of mere 'theory' or to being 'just about words' is intended, more or less unconsciously, to get it out of the way so that the relegator can then get on with his compulsive concerns.

My feeling (it is difficult to produce empirical evidence) is that neither of these two ideas gives us the whole story. At a certain level – a level both of the conscious mind and of the reactions themselves, as these latter are expressed in conversation – the layman may feel only baffled, irritated, impatient or frankly bored. But at a slightly deeper level, after the conversation has continued for a few minutes and something of what the philosopher is about may have become plainer, if only in general outline (as a cloud looms on the horizon), what he feels is a certain kind of *alarm*. My guess, dramatic though it sounds, is that the alarm is about the possibility not that what he or some other person says may be wrong – that is (barely) tolerable, and he can always bite back – but that it *makes no sense*. The way in which conceptual analysis can undercut (not oppose) what people say, familiar enough to philosophers, is when glimpsed extremely alarming. It is as if, not this or that tree or building were under fire or destroyed, but the whole foundation of the earth on which one stood were shaking in a seismic tremor. It is not as if one or the other element in a person's ideology or system of beliefs were under attack, but rather as if the whole system were in danger of being shown up as a kind of dream or fantasy.

In psychotherapy the patient clings to certain ideas or fantasies which are not just mistakes (as measured against the real world), but which are internally incoherent and contain irreconcilable elements. For example, he wants to be very close to another person because he needs love and security, but he also wants to be detached because he is frightened of being smothered and needs to preserve his independence: so he moves in and out of relationships with great rapidity, driven back and forth from one element to the other and finding no rest. Or again, he wants to prove his power over another person (so that the person must be free, otherwise his power is unproven), yet because he doubts that power the person must be tied up and under his control; so he acts, out, like de Sade, a succession of scenes which represent the nearest he can get to incorporating both elements at once. There are many parallels here which emerge in philosophy. The egalitarian ideologue relies on the continued existence of certain differentials between people (otherwise there would be nothing to be egalitarian *about*), but at the same time is frightened of differences because (or ostensibly because) they may be put into the service of tyranny or prejudice: he finds himself obliged to advocate a certain homogeneity, from which (as in totalitarian countries) new differentials of course arise. The relativist ideologue cannot tolerate authority or objective reason in ethics, but at the same time needs to continue acting and choosing as a human being: and is thus driven to locate the authority, as existentialists frenetically if ambivalently seek to do, in some obscure part of himself. There are in fact no egalitarians who really want everyone to be treated the same or to be the same as everyone else, and no relativists who really want choice to be arbitrary: it is not that they hold some extreme or mistaken theory. It is rather that they feel themselves obliged to hold together two warring elements.

What alarms the layman, like the patient, is not that the philosopher may prove him wrong: indeed he may have no real conceptual grasp of what 'proving someone wrong' means in philosophy. It is not even that the philosopher will take away some unreal but coherent dream or fantasy, though this is often the case. It is rather that he feels the philosopher may uncover the irreconcilable elements, both of which are necessary to his mental security, and show them to be irreconcilable – or not to be reconciled in the way he has to date preferred. When this is shown, he feels himself desperate. He may admit to being wrong, since he can be right next time: he can give up a dream, since he can dream another dream later on: but if he feels very deeply that he must have both A and B, and B is shown to be *logically* inconsistent with A – not just contingently inconsistent, as if by herculean efforts he might somehow get both – then there seems to be no way out.

I hope to have said enough to show that some, at least, of the layman's reactions to philosophy have fairly deep pathological roots. There would not be much point in showing this, and in describing them, if I did not think it possible to achieve a cure. But because the roots *are* deep, it is not clear how much can really be achieved by methods of teaching philosophy which do not recreate something of the relationship between therapist and patient. Something, no doubt, perhaps for many people a great deal, can be achieved just by practice and a certain amount of external pressure (from examinations, for instance): and I do not at all suggest that the teacher of philosophy immediately turns his classes into one or another brand of confessional therapy. Moreover, trust and the right sort of (non-prurient) intimacy can be built up on the side, as it were, in the course of teacher and pupils jointly pursuing some other aim – philosophical truth itself, perhaps. But in practice this does not too often happen: what happens is that philosophy rarely 'takes', even though we may persuade students to go through the motions.

I say 'students', but of course there is just as much or more difficulty with one's non-philosophical colleagues (who are not even, and do not want to be, students of philosophy). There are ways of building up trust and a coherent working group if one is dealing with pupils under authority, and pupils young enough not to have evolved impregnable defences for their psychological vested interests. Adult academics, perhaps particularly in departments (faculties, schools, etc.) of education and other institutions that are generally *mal vu*, do not commonly display the trust, friendliness, self-confidence and enthusiasm for truth outside their own specialism which are necessary if philosophy, in particular, is to get off the ground and overcome the pathological reactions mentioned earlier. This depressing fact has to be faced: as we must also face the fact that philosophers themselves are hardly paragons in respect of these virtues. This would matter less if they were not – as in education they are bound to be – in the position of missionaries. Like it or not (and most philosophers do not), public relations – in a broad sense of that phrase – are a central feature of the missionary's work: and unless the philosopher takes that seriously, accusations about ivory towers are plausible. There are, surely, many ways in which serious philosophers can at least try to overcome these difficulties, in answer to the question "How, given these obstacles (and no doubt others), can philosophy be best institutionalised or facilitated?" I am not aware of much serious work on this question: and what I have said above may help only by highlighting some of the problems. Almost everything remains to be done.

Besides (and because of) an understanding of psychological reactions to philosophy, we badly need a proper social context for teaching it: one which is sufficiently informal and generates sufficient trust for the business to go well. Any kind of rational argument, and *a fortiori* philosophical or conceptual argument, is a highly skilled business: few people take to it naturally, and the relevant abilities and attitudes have to be carefully and systematically encouraged. In particular the participants must get to know (and trust) each other well, which means – at least to begin with – in contexts where some other activity (preferably simpler and more initially attractive than philosophy) is shared.

The point raises, however, a sharp challenge to most systems of education, which rely on highly mechanical and bureaucratised contexts: set classes in bleak buildings, formal assignments, impersonal procedures, rigid hours, even sometimes 'behavioural objectives'. Philosophy can be institutionalised, but most of our present institutions do not suit it. We have to remodel our institutions round the Socratic idea of a *person* who is (informally as well as formally) responsible for a large part of the lives and thinking of other people: someone more like a parent, or *in loco parentis*, than like an instructor. This involves trusting the philosopher with far more responsibility than most societies are at present willing to give him. The same goes for any teacher: for even in subjects which require less dialectical discussion and more factual information the information can be gleaned more effectively from books and other mechanical sources – a *teacher* is only needed because we need a *person* even in these (factual) subjects. There may be more need for a personal teacher in some subjects that others, though actually I suspect it is rather that the need is different in different subjects; but the general point here is relevant to all subjects, and all education – not just to philosophy.

At the same time, and ultimately for the same reasons, no social or institutional change by itself will achieve very much, unless the teachers of philosophy make a much more serious effort to understand and practise what the teaching of the subject demands. We saw in the last chapter that we have good reason not to fall in with those (many) people who claim philosophy, viewed as a practical method of change, to be ineffective and Utopian, inefficient and slow when compared with (say) propaganda or politics: the point being simply that for changing some kinds of things, philosophy is positively necessary – the change cannot be made by other methods. But there is another claim which is much more telling: the claim that, whilst philosophy is indeed necessary as a method, the method cannot be deployed because certain preconditions have not been satisfied. Briefly, the idea is not that people do not need philosophy, but that they are not (for the most part) able to engage in it unless certain other things are done first.

In this general form such a claim would be obviously true but boring: it is clear, for instance, that if people are starving or on the rack they are unlikely to go in much for philosophy. There is a whole range of preconditions for anything: we cannot even teach children to read unless they are reasonably well-fed, sitting in above-zero temperatures, and so forth. However, one version of the claim has a special interest for us: the idea that philosophy or philosophising is very closely intertwined, both in practice and in theory, with certain other features or capacities of the human mind. It is rather as if we said that somebody could not do, say, advanced physics unless he could first, or also, do mathematics; and that might be a rather more interesting claim than the claim that he could not do advanced physics if he were dreaming or suffering from violent toothache.

The claim might have two forms: (1) in which these other capacities were, genuinely to be seen as preconditions of doing philosophy, either (a) as a matter of fact (it just happened to be the case that these capacities were needed), or (b) as a matter of logic (it is logical, not a contingent, precondition of playing chess properly that one has learned the moves of individual pieces). Alternatively, (2) the claim might be that philosophy, if closely inspected, could be seen itself to involve these capacities, not as preconditions to be satisfied beforehand, but as part of philosophising itself; and here again we could see this involvement as either (2(a)) factual, or (2(b)) logical.

I have so far spoken of 'capacities' or 'features' without filling in the blanks, because which version of the claim we take up will plainly depend on how we do fill in the blanks, as well as on how we construe 'philosophy'. Characteristically philosophers, perhaps anxious to dissociate themselves from any idea that they should act as sages, moralists, doctors or spiritual leaders, have (at least in the fairly recent past) been at pains to distinguish philosophy from those practices designed to improve mental health – we may use 'psychotherapy' as a shorthand for these, on the understanding that we are not talking about the use of drugs and other physical methods, but (roughly) about talk between therapist and patient designed to improve the patient's rationality and sanity. Hence, unsurprisingly, they have construed a minimum level of rationality or sanity as a precondition or *sine qua non* for philosophy, and by this separation kept philosophy pure and (as some might see it) uncorrupted by psychotherapeutic considerations.

Despite Wittgenstein's persistent remarks to the effect that philosophy is a battle against the bewitchment of our intelligence by language, a similar kind of separatism is observable in his work (and life: he did not allow the idea that there was something *wrong* with his emotional state to conjoin with the idea that there might be people, even if stupider than he, whom he could trust over a long period of time to help him). Indeed the whole notion that it is *language* which bewitches our intelligence, though this is (or used to be) a commonplace of philosophical procedure, is in fact rather a strange one as it stands: as if the grammatical forms alone, or mysterious phrases such as 'not but what', or the ease with which classical Greek forms abstract nouns from adjectives, or whatever, was in itself sufficient explanation for centuries of philosophical puzzlement, or even for the feeling of being trapped or uncertain which he so well describes and illustrates. Of course not: either the linguistic form exists as a result of certain psychically potent temptations, or at least it would be harmless if those temptations did not make use of it. By the pompous phrase 'psychically potent', I mean only that we must be able to show how and why the various tendencies to think in this or that way, or to get muddled up in such-and-such a manner, are in fact attractive to human beings.

Nor, fairly obviously, is this by any means an impossible task. It is not too hard to see (at least in a general sort of way) why, for instance, people find it attractive to believe in the absence of any kind of rules or authority, or construe abstract nouns as if they were the names of things, or for long considered moral arguments to be essentially similar to factual ones, or sought for other areas of discourse the kind of certainty we find in geometry. We do not have to be trained psychoanalysts to recognise these and similar points. But if we take seriously the suggestion that, where there is philosophical muddle or doubt, there is likely to be some form of attraction that has led to that muddle or doubt, then we shall also have to take seriously the suggestion that (as in psychotherapy) there is bound to be some *resistance* to clearing up the muddle or doubt, because we shall be trying to remove something the patient (pupil) wants to keep. The resistance will not be just that pupils are often stupid or bloody-minded (so that the philosopher needs only the usual patience and tact of any teacher); but the philosopher's efforts will, essentially, run up against the pupil's desires and fantasies.

The kind of realism (if that is the right word) which Thrasymachus displays in Plato's *Republic*, and which has been often displayed by later thinkers – particularly by those of a sociological turn of mind in recent years – has here some force:

though not quite the force claimed by those who advance it. "Whatever you may say about the concepts, *in practice*" (heavy emphasis) "justice (or mental health or whatever) is defined by those in power." Similarly we might say "Although in theory (as it were, transcendentally) you can draw a distinction between philosophy and psychotherapy – philosophy involves exhibiting conceptual truths whereas psychotherapy does not (though in fact it does in a way) – nevertheless *in practice* one has to exhibit these truths, or (more obviously) exhibit incoherencies, *against a certain background*: and in fact this background will be one in which the pupil and indeed the philosopher himself are fighting against their tendencies to fantasy". We might add, as Thrasymacheans and Marxists would not, (1) that this was not just an empirical (sociological) or contingent point, but that there were conceptual reasons (that is, reasons explicable from the concepts marked by 'person', 'growing up', 'developing a mind', etc.) why men were liable to fantasy in this way, and why they would resist clarity; and (2) that this provided a strong reason, not for abandoning philosophy in favour of sociology or politics, or some other kind of empirical analysis or movement, but for doing philosophy harder – though, perhaps, more successfully now that we recognise some aspects of the opposition.

I am not saying (a) that 'philosophy' and 'psychotherapy' (or 'a struggle against fantasy', or even ' . . . fantasy as it emerges in language') should be regarded as equivalent in meaning; nor (b) that philosophy consists *only* of the sort of work in which fantasy is our opponent – there may well be many areas and problems, fairly to be called 'philosophical', where fantasy does not get in the way at all. Nevertheless I should still want to maintain, as hinted above, that it is not a purely contingent fact that we run up against fantasy when doing philosophy – particularly perhaps, or perhaps just most obviously, in certain areas such as moral and political philosophy, philosophy of education and of religion, and some others. Certainly in practice, and given men as they are likely to be for the foreseeable future, and at least for certain (very important) kinds of or topics in philosophy, the connection is a very strong one.

When people disagree, it is not or not only because they are stupid or logically imperceptive. It is because they are trying to say something which, they often feel, has not had a fair hearing: they are trying to point to some good with which they are, as it were, in close emotional contact, but which they cannot see clearly and describe properly. They do not know what it is exactly that they are trying to say, but they know it is important and not easily done justice to by any very quick piece of philosophising. In this they are often quite right; and philosophers are often much to be blamed for not trying hard enough, or skilfully enough, to elicit it. For unless a person's feelings – if only as they emerge in language – are not done justice to, he will almost certainly deny or evade any conceptual points that philosophers may put to him. This is true of all of us, even – in some respects, particularly – of philosophers themselves.

One might put this by saying that unless philosophy (conceptual analysis, is mixed with a little psychotherapy (psychological analysis) it is not likely to be of much use: but I would ultimately reject this description, because I think that some forms of philosophy and of psychotherapy, or some aspects of them, are in fact identical. Thus if we consider, Socratically, just what someone is saying or trying to say, how can we possibly do this without some kind of investigation into why he wants to say it? And conversely, if we are considering, psychologically, why someone says (or does) something, how can we do this without a clear conceptual account of just what the words (actions) mean? There is, of course, much more to be said about this; but my belief is that many apparently irreconcileable differences at a philosophical or an ideological level could be sorted out without too much difficulty, provided that the parties concerned were willing to examine their own motives in a manner slightly more profound than is usual in an orthodox philosophy tutorial. The distinction between "Is it true that . . . ?" and "Why, psychologically, do you want to say that . . . ?", which might be thought to mark the difference between philosophy and psychological enquiry or therapy, is difficult and perhaps ultimately impossible to sustain. As I have tried to show elsewhere, (Wilson, 1979b) there is at least a case for trying to combine a strictly logical enquiry with some understanding of the fantasies that lie beneath (and not so far beneath) a great deal of talk on most topics to which philosophy is relevant.

Any practical programme to this effect would require –

amongst other things, but perhaps most obviously – a considerable increase in the degree of *trust* between teacher and pupil. This would merit a whole book in itself: here I will confine myself to mentioning two doctrinaire ideas which it is essential to avoid. The first, associated (perhaps too readily) with certain practices now popular in some circles, is to assume that trust can be generated quickly and easily by certain overt moves – physical embraces, direct confession, totally unguarded speech, and a kind of ritualised or routinised self-propulsion towards other people. The trouble with this is (a) that to *some* extent trust cannot be hurried but takes time; (b) that the moves and practices are likely to be insincere, superficial and in an important sense artificial or clinical – one is not trusted idiosyncratically but as some (any) person needing 'care' and 'concern' and 'sympathy' and so on; and of course (c) that barriers may be breached too soon, causing pain and distrust that could have been avoided. On the other hand, there is a second doctrinaire idea (much more common in the UK and other older countries) that *any* conscious attempt to penetrate barriers and accelerate trust must be bogus and/or offensive to people's sense of privacy. As stated, of course, that idea is clearly ridiculous: nobody, however stuffy, is opposed to shaking hands or sharing drinks. Nevertheless, sometimes the idea acts as a dogmatic piece of conservatism, so that the person will not go out of his way to seek methods of improving trust (or even face the problem squarely at all), and is likely to resist on principle new-fangled methods intended to do so. A person dominated by this idea, particularly if he is paid to teach and communicate, has a bad case of *mauvaise foi*.

Another problem connects with this: briefly, the extent to which the teacher focuses the group's general attention (a) outwards (upon philosophical problems themselves, or in the course of warming-up or trust-inducing exercises upon some other external goal or task); or (b) inwards, upon the particular psychic states of the individuals, in so far as these need inspection and discussion in order to improve their philosophical thinking. I have discussed this elsewhere (Wilson, 1979b, p. 4ff.) taking the view that (a) certainly cannot be the complete answer; but I do not think it a problem with a single determinate solution – much obviously depends on the individuals concerned, including the teacher. It would be instructive, if we had space and time, to consider cases; for instance, what would be required to deal properly with a Thresymachus (of course he can be *silenced*, but does that really help him?). I incline to think that (b) is underplayed, partly because we do not know how to conduct psychotherapy effectively (particularly if we are untrained amateurs) and partly because we are frightened by muddling it up too much with philosophy – both excellent reasons, but not in all cases decisive. Perhaps we shall be clearer with the help of further research: for now, I can plead only for a recognition of the problem.

These (rather slight) remarks obviously owe much to what philosophers from Plato to Wittgenstein seem to want some-times to say: but I reject, of course, the idea that 'philosophy leaves everything as it is', if by 'everything' we include our own understanding, or our own acceptance of the conceptual struc-tures we now have. On the contrary: I think it would appear – as it very clearly appears in psychotherapy – that much of what we now say and do is largely unreal, evasive, distorted and (unsurprisingly) logically incoherent. That would be all the more probable if, as I also believe, men are landed with a set of broadly-defined standard interests which they often see only in a distorted or symbolic form: as a miser can appreciate the standard interest of security only if he hoards and runs his fingers through his gold, or a sadist the standard interest of power only by setting out his desire for power in extreme and bizarre forms. But equally, if even the most bizarre words and deeds can, with sufficient patience and insight, be brought within the fold of acceptable (and perhaps inevitable or 'given') human concerns, we may reasonably hope that ideo-logical and other contests are not really, as some philosophers delight in insisting, 'irresolvable', 'permanently disputable', or 'endless'. It might also present a rather different picture to that which many philosophers in our own day have painted: the suggestions (a) that men are *au fond* very different from each other, and (b) that there is no reason to believe that all values are assimilable into some single Good Life – in a word, the strong reaction against any kind of monistic rationalism which is characteristic of our age, at least in liberal societies – , whilst they clearly have force, many seem less obviously true if one believes that many human differences, including different per-ceptions of apparently conflicting or non-assimilable values, may be due to different kinds of alienation from our standard interests. In other words, we are so very bad at knowing ourselves and what is good for ourselves that we are not yet entitled to adopt a pluralist rather than a monistic view.

Many readers will still feel, with some justice, that I have been far too vague in making positive pedagogic suggestions about how, in practice, we should go about teaching philosophy. So I will end this chapter by putting down – too briefly and still too sketchily, but I hope at least clearly – a number of fairly practical suggestions which might at least start off some serious research in this area.

(1)   The first point is itself philosophical or at any rate meth-odological. Research on methods of teaching a subject S must be conducted by a researcher who is himself reason-ably expert in S. This is obvious enough: the question of what *other* qualifications he needs is harder, for it de-pends on the type of obstacles to learning S that one believes to exist. Thus in some countries there may be political obstacles to a discussion of (say) the rightness or wrongness of what Marx or Mao or St Paul wrote. These aside, there remain questions about the sort of 'psycho-logical' (if this word may do duty for what is left over in a situation where political or social factors at least permit discussion) difficulties that inhibit discussion. Are we to look, for instance, only at the basic fantasies and uncon-scious prejudices of the discussers – for which we should need a clinical psychologist or psychiatrist? Or at various aspects of their social interaction – the way the chairs are placed, etc. – in which case a social psychologist would be our man? Clearly there is no single right answer to such questions; it seems to me that serious research could only be conducted by a small team of people who covered all the relevant ground.

(2)   Such a team's first task, or a task for the philosopher in it, would be to spell out what was meant by some such phrase as 'doing philosophy well'. I shall take it here that we are not primarily concerned with historical or empiri-cal knowledge, but with initiating people into a certain

way of thinking and encouraging the development of certain abilities and types of awareness in them: the word 'conceptual' may stand as an overall description here, but any competent philosopher can fill this out for himself. (And even if different philosophers fill it out somewhat differently, there is a consensus of practice from Socrates onwards.) To this should, in my view, be added some notion of the pupils *wanting* to do it and to do it well, and of philosophy becoming an important part of their (present and future) *lives*: that is, not a game, but something they become and remain serious about. It would be as important for a researcher to assess this as to assess pupils' actual skills or abilities.

(3) This last point would reinforce the notion of philosophy as essentially a matter of dialogue. Dialogue is possible in one's own head, in talk with one's fellows, and on paper (A writes an article to which B replies by another article); but the second of these seems crucial here. For most people internal dialogue can only be learned by enough practice in external dialogue which is then internalised; and the written dialogue, in itself cumbersome, also requires a good deal of sophistication. I shall take it, then, that the (or at least a) central concern is to get pupils to like, be good at, and take seriously, philosophical discussion. (The Socratic dialogues are again our model.) This does not imply that they should not write things down on paper (see below); but it implies that oral dispute is an essential starting-point.

(4) It must now be recognised that such discussion is *extremely sophisticated* and immensely difficult to learn. Most people cannot conduct an effective discussion about anything, let alone philosophy. To some extent the rules for discussion can be identified and straightforwardly taught and practised (I have made some suggestions about this elsewhere: Wilson, 1971b), and this certainly needs doing: it is something any normal child ought to have been taught by the time he is, say, 15 at the latest. Nevertheless there remain very general psychological difficulties, particularly in philosophical discussion, not all of which can be easily overcome by teaching and

practice – though a lot can: one can, and should, simply
drill people into talking clearly, neither too briefly nor at
too great a length, neither too aggressively nor too
unenthusiastically, and so on. And this itself does a lot to
overcome nerves, impatience, boredom and other such.
But it is not enough.

(5) These general psychological obstacles, as I see them, can
be roughly categorised under two headings: first, a lack
of trust in the members of the group; and second, the
compulsive power of various fantasies. Here I can only
suggest a number of methods designed to overcome or
palliate these (or at least render them recognisable to
pupils), which I have used and which seem to work:

(i) Put the group, before starting to discuss at all, in a
trust-inducing context: for instance, a simple context
which involves them physically and enjoyably a
game, a party, swimming, camping together, sharing
food and drink. There is some added advantage if the
context makes them *work* together as well as enjoy
themselves.

(ii) Make sure that, both during this process *and* in the
actual philosophy teaching, the time they are together
is long enough. A weekend is much better than the
equivalent number of hours spread throughout a
term.

(iii) So far as possible, try to identify the particular fears,
fantasies and other temptations to irrelevance or philosophical incompetence that the pupils have *before*
starting to do serious philosophy.

(iv) Give them some practice at identifying these in other
people's talk and writings, and subsequently in their
own.

(v) Distinguish the times and contexts in which you are
doing (i)–(iv) above very sharply from those in which
you are doing serious philosophy: do not let there be
a muddle between philosophy and the *ad hominem*
stuff which is more appropriate for a psychotherapy
group. Reach a position where you can say, in effect
"Right, now we know and trust each other and have

some idea about our temptations to fantasy in various directions, we'll do some serious *work*." One can then be much more crisp and waste less time.

(6)   Remembering still that philosophical discussion is a very sophisticated activity, and assuming that we are all the time drilling and initiating the pupils into the rules of effective discussion, we shall want to pitch the philosophy pretty low to begin with. It is wise not to take difficult and long-standing philosophical problems, but to get the pupils well-trained in simple conceptual discourse. Let A suggest a definition, and B immediately suggest a counter-example. This is, I believe, the only way to cut out the vast swathes of irrelevant first-order talk that will otherwise go on, and perhaps prevent most pupils from ever coming to see what philosophy is about: the only way of making it absolutely clear that we do *not* want empirical facts, moral or political or religious beliefs, or general chit-chat, but insist on attention to concepts.

(7)   This is the first and most crucial stage. When – only when – they have got the hang of this, the rest is in principle easy. One can use tape-recorders, replaying a discussion to detect irrelevancies: very short oral statements, prepared beforehand, and replied to by another prepared statement: a single written page read out, answered during the next session by another single page – and so on. One has constantly to resist the temptation to go too fast; but in the early stages – which last a long time and are more than half the battle – anything like a long essay, or a thesis, or a long speech will certainly be autistic and largely irrelevant to serious philosophical analysis. (Because of autism, setting passages for pupils' criticism is better than asking for their own views: a useful exercise is to get them to criticise their own past statements.)

(8)   I by no means imply that reading books is useless. For beginners to read long and difficult books usually *is* useless, and does no more than encourage them to set philosophy aside and turn to whatever contemporary sages may be fashionable. But there are various introductions to philosophy which may be worth using, though

many such are far too difficult. Here I would want to stress the importance of allowing pupils to choose the style or lay-out of such introductions that suit their own taste – provided the alternatives are all philosophically satisfactory. If I may use a personal example (and not for self-advertisement): I have written three very different introductions to philosophical thinking, two chiefly out of dissatisfaction with the one before. One of these (Wilson, 1956) tries to set out different kinds of words, statements and truth, in a cut-and-dried way (grotesquely oversimplified): another (1963) tries to give the reader some idea of and practice in the skills of conceptual analysis: the third (1968) simply discusses, very informally, some popular problems ("What is a work of art?" etc.). The odd fact is that different pupils quite evidently profit from these very different approaches: some find the first book intolerable, others can only benefit from the third, and so on. The merits or demerits of the books *per se* are here irrelevant: for some reason different styles, lay-outs, or approaches fit different temperaments. No doubt other philosophers have similar experiences: we must do the best we can.

6 Reactions to Reason

It falls to the philosopher – rather than the scientist, or the linguist, or the representatives of most other disciplines (not all: literature and certain brands of social science, to name but two, suffer the same fate) – to encounter not just the specific reactions to philosophy mentioned above, but a general profession of irrationalism. Usually and predictably this happens when he is discussing something close to the human heart: religion, or personal relations, or something of that kind – not formal logic or the existence of tables. Something has to be said about this, since not much is gained if we cure our specific hostility to philosophy only to fall into a more general hostility to reason. Of course this is an enormous topic: I make here only a few points that I think have been missed or underemphasised.

Protests against the reasonable man are often too quickly aborted. For (we may argue) if something is *right*, or desirable, or good, or whatever, then there must be some *reason* why it is right: and we want people who will act in accordance with that reason. This seems to hold for anything: it may sometimes, perhaps often, be right to kiss or smite rather than argue, start a revolution rather than a negotiation, follow one's instincts rather than one's calculations, and in general act spontaneously rather than as a result of ratiocination. Very well: if so, then these are reasonable things to do, and the reasonable man will do them. That is sound enough, but runs too quickly past the different kind of protests that can fairly be made.

Imagine a man with a certain concept of happiness in marriage or personal relationships generally, framed more in terms of contentment and stability than in terms of romance and passion. He usually thinks things out and acts, according to his lights, with prudence and good sense. His wife appears, dressed (undressed) to kill, when the dinner is cooking and he is in the middle of some work. He takes the view that there is a

132

time and a place for everything, and that passion should be delayed lest the dinner burn or the train of thought is lost: she says "Oh, stop being so reasonable!" She may have in mind (1) that he really ought not to be ratiocinating at all about this, but ought just to grab her (and never mind the consequences); and/or (2) that he is ratiocinating inefficiently – that, even on his own concept of happiness, the loss of well-cooked dinner or train of thought would be well worth it. Often it is hard to distinguish these. If he who bends to himself a joy does the winged life destroy, whereas he who kisses the joy as it flies lives in eternity's sunrise, then does the mere process of ratiocination count as bending to himself? Or is it all right to think a bit, so long as one comes to the right conclusion? Perhaps it turns on how, and how much, he thinks. But both these are different from (3) the objection that he has a mistakenly narrow idea of happiness. Suppose his will prevails: the dinner is cooked and eaten, the train of thought completed: passion follows, only it is somehow not very wild. It is wild enough (so he believes) for him: he thinks he is happy and that all is well. But he may be wrong. Here we might say that he is reasonable enough for what he – the conscious part of him – is: but that there is not enough of him in his consciousness.

Prudent people (including prudent philosophers) are likely to start from the idea, perfectly sound so far as it goes, that in human affairs things are apt to go badly. But other people, not necessarily lacking all concept of prudence, may start from a different idea: that things are even more apt to go boringly. What seems dreadful to them is not so much the misuse of human desires, but the denial of them. Philosophers (unless you count people like Nietzsche) are apt to overlook this or hurry too quickly past it. Much of the protest against being reasonable is because reason is seen as essentially *adjudicating* between desires, suggesting the repression of some and legitimation of others, generating rules and principles on the tacit assumption that all the evidence or all the subject-matter is on the map, already visible. But (we protest) it is not: much, perhaps most, of it is hidden.

We have then to underline here the idea that reason *enables* as well as adjudicates. Nor does it only enable the adoption of some system or arrangement which is wiser, or more prudent, or more just: philosophers' constant concern with justice again

suggests that we know well enough what the goods are which
we have to be just about, that the content of human interests is
sufficiently clear for us to spend most of our time in negotiating
them. Of course in some degree this is true. But we need also
to stress the role of reason in eliciting or unearthing interests
which are hidden from us, or which emerge only in brute forms
(for instance, uncontrolled violence). Reason enables us to
know ourselves, not just to adjudicate what is already known.

It is in a way strange that this should have to be said, since
we are entirely familiar with many forms of activity which
attempt such a task. When engaged in writing or reading a
novel, or in some kind of psychotherapy, or even in ordinary
conversation or reflection about personal matters, we *think*,
perceive, describe, even in some sense argue. The mere acting
out of brute impulses teaches us nothing: we have to negotiate
and adjudicate, in our own minds and with the help of others,
simply in order to find out what lies hidden, what we are
missing, what we have misdescribed. That is no less a form of
reasoning than mathematics or philosophy or scientific enquiry. Nor are the rules less stringent: they are just different.

We might rephrase the protest by saying that we want not
just a *reasonable* man, but a reasonable *man* (not a reasonable
mouse, or robot, or role-player). The protest is not against
reason as such – that makes no sense – but against the misuse
of reason: against its operation on too narrow a front, or on
subject-matter too poor to be of much use. There is a sort of
parallel with the protest against armchair science or (if there is
such a thing) armchair archaeology: there are not enough facts
to reason about if you just sit in the armchair and think – one
has to go out and look (dig). We should not (it might be said)
conduct long and sterile theological, perhaps not even philosophical, arguments; since these plainly get off the ground only
because certain psychological moves have already been made
which the disputants themselves are unaware of, and which
they cannot hope to grasp unless they step back from the
dispute and direct their gaze elsewhere – probably inwards. It
is easy enough to be reasonable as a theologian, or as a
suburban husband, or as a bureaucrat, or in any other of the
roles which take certain ends and rules as given: to be reasonable as a man is more difficult.

The desirability of applying reason to life as an overall policy is something which cannot be coherently denied – that is, so long as the notions of reason and being reasonable are interpreted in a broad enough sense to do justice to normal usage. It is often reasonable not to ratiocinate: to follow hunches, impulses, or superstitions: to govern oneself, and allow others to be governed, by motives and beliefs which do not under analysis stand up as justifications but which nevertheless keep our behaviour on the right lines. But *some* application of reason, some weighing of evidence and reflection, is required even to make this claim plausible. There must still be *somebody* – if not ourselves, then our fathers or priests or rulers or psychiatrists – to make various judgements, and to have good grounds for making them. And this means that *somewhere* there must be a context in which certain people try to learn what these 'good grounds' are, and how they apply to particular cases: which is all that the enterprise of philosophical education requires.

I do not deny (having myself been frequently guilty) that philosophers and educators of what might be roughly called a 'liberal' turn of mind have often spoken misleadingly, naively, and over-optimistically on this matter. It is always an open question, and very largely an empirical one, just how, how much, when, by whom, where, etc. this context of rational consideration and discussion should be brought into play. To assume that it should always be brought into play by everybody is as grotesque as assuming that the best way of dealing with savages, lunatics or young children is always to argue with them or try to educate them. Increase in understanding is *one* good, and a very important one: but there are others. The opponents of Socrates had or could have had a case, whatever their actual motives: even if he improved the understanding of Athens' young citizens, he may also have made them less able or less willing to preserve social cohesion and defend their country in time of war. Similarly it is understandable that Plato believed dialectical philosophy to be wasted on, and dangerous for, those who were too young to use it properly.

It is tempting to suggest that many liberal thinkers have been led to interpret reason too narrowly, and to put too much money on the narrow interpretation – that is, to insist on an excessive or inopportune use of a context of ratiocination, learning and discussion – because they themselves found non-

rational contexts and pressures intolerable for personal reasons, and invested heavily in contexts of ratiocination as (for
them) the only way of preserving some kind of identity and
personal integration. We have to accept, what is indeed wholly
obvious, that individuals and societies for the most part preserve their identity and psychic security for reasons that have
little to do with what is true, right or justifiable, except perhaps
per accidens; and that the improper introduction of 'open'
contexts – contexts in which people are supposed to follow
'wherever the argument may lead' – may have bad effects. One
result may be to shatter or at least disturb the myths on which
their identity and happiness (even their sanity) may rest:
another, to entrench them more firmly and paranoiacally
within these myths. That is why, as I have been at pains to
stress earlier, such contexts are for the most part useless or
positively destructive unless backed by a sufficient degree of
trust and love.

An obsession with these contexts, by blinding such thinkers
to the existence of other goods, blinds them also to the importance of non-rational properties which are often necessary
preconditions for attaining them. There is, for instance, a
certain irony in launching high-minded programmes of moral
education at a time when many teachers in many schools have
no power to control their pupils adequately even in simple
ways: when, indeed, our own and other liberal societies are
unable or unwilling to prevent serious forms of crime, delin-
quency and social disorder, sometimes amounting to not much
less than civil war. It is as if we thought that to behave
reasonably was always to behave in some tender-minded,
non-aggressive way. But that is, of course, to abandon any
kind of rational control over a large part of ourselves, by
denying the existence of that part. There are times when we
need to discuss and ratiocinate as equals: but there are also
times when we need to issue crisp orders and make sure they
are obeyed – even, perhaps, times when we need to bring in
the tanks and clear the streets.

The important thing, as always, is simply to *distinguish*.
What goes wrong when a society is more or less totally involved in some myth or partisan picture is obvious enough:
there is *nowhere* for such contexts to flourish, because every
context (even in the universities) is dominated by the myth.

When the myth begins to collapse, it collapses through non-negotiated and largely unseen social pressures, not as a result of intelligent and properly-understood criticism – because such criticism is not institutionalised anywhere, or is not properly diffused through the society. On the other hand, when the contexts are over-employed (often under fashionable titles like 'participation', 'democracy' and so on), the goods sustained by the myth – and these will include some sort of cohesion and order – begin to be eroded: for the contexts will be largely used for critical and not constructive purposes – often for the benefit of a personal vendetta on the part of those who find the myth psychologically intolerable. Only a fairly sharp distinction, made both in theory and in institutional practice, between contexts of free discussion and learning on the one hand and contexts where the aim is to get something done on the other will save us from this sort of chaos.

It would be rash to expect that any society, in the near future at least, will be able to preserve its cohesion and flexibility by providing a socially effective form of philosophical education which is also intellectually respectable. We may confidently if unwillingly expect a continuation of the cycles in which cohesion is maintained by some form of irrational myth that collapses only to be replaced after a period of chaos by some other form. The pressures are too strong to hope otherwise: and they have nowhere been seriously counteracted by any rational attempt at such education in the past, so that when the myth and consensus breaks down there will be no solid bed-rock of reason or common sense beyond which our affairs cannot sink. It may be that the best we can do is to maintain and defend some isolated pockets in which the idea, and perhaps to some degree the practice, of such education will be preserved through the tyrannies and anarchies of the future. That is to paint a dramatic picture; but it may fit the facts. If the facts turn out to be more benevolent, so much the better.

There is one respect, indeed, in which the position is not quite so desperate as one might suppose. Men are not irredeemably selfish and ineducable: the kind of thing that goes wrong is not something brute and unmanageable, like an earthquake. It is, of course, a fact that men have limited sympathies and are selfish: and not a merely contingent fact either, since there are unalterable reasons why the progress from autism or egocentr-

icity to altruism or fraternity is fraught with difficulty for any
rational creature. Nevertheless it is also a fact that men feel a
strong need to justify what they do and how they feel: not only
in public, but also to themselves. Cases in which men overtly
glory in what they know to be, and describe to themselves and
others as, bad or evil are extremely rare: which is why they
strike us as not just monstrous but peculiar whether they make
a philosophy out of it or just wallow in it like Aaron (*Titus
Andronicus*, V.i. 123ff.). Of course some philosophers will
make so close a connection between what one (really, sin-
cerely) thinks good and what one actually does that such cases
will be not only rare but impossible; but even without making
this move, we can see how deep-rooted is the desire to see
what one does as in some way *all right*, as brought under some
syllogism whose premisses are somehow acceptable. Usually
one tries to justify the action in a strong sense – it is for the
sake of the Party, or to fulfil one's destiny, or in the other
person's best interests, or whatever: failing that, one may try to
make it justifiable at least from a particular point of view ("As
a Christian, I had to . . ."), or as in accord with some kind of
principle ("Well, he deserved it"), or at worst understandable
and forgivable ("I was sorely provoked").

We may usefully ask why this is so; and the answer is not, I
think, entirely to be given in terms of saving face in front of
other men, or even of keeping one's own conscience quiet (if
'conscience' is taken in the rather specific, as it were Protes-
tant, sense of internalised guilt). It is rather that I have to see
myself as good, and also as reasonable in my dealings, if I am
to have confidence in my continued existence in a public world:
if I am to be a rational being at all aiming at goods and
following principles. It is not a matter of 'morality' so much as
of sanity: just as a respect for truth – not just truthfulness to
others – is necessary to avoid lunacy or at least extreme autism.
By being untruthful we may get black looks from our neighbours: but if we turn a completely blind eye to truth, to the
facts, to what is the case and what is not, then we run the risk
of total isolation and excommunication. Hence we cling to the
ideas of believing only on evidence, of justification, of at least
appearing to abide by the public rules. With our actions it is the
same: indeed, both are aspects of the general necessity to

retain our (publicly-demonstrated and public-dependent) identity. We feel that we must at least put up a show.

It is perhaps worth adding that even our repentance and
admissions of guilt tend to be either half-hearted or autistic.
Either, that is, we say "Yes, it was wrong but . . ." (and here
follows some special pleading or mitigation): or else, less
obviously, we *predetermine* (usually unconsciously) what we
are going to feel guilty about, and then play out a drama of
acknowledged wickedness and repentance which is autistic at
least in the sense that it is designed to make ourselves feel
better rather than actually to correct our perceptions or attitudes. In this (very common) mood we rarely make effective
reparation to any injured party, or take steps to re-educate
ourselves so that it does not happen again, or sharpen our
perceptions and descriptions of the world so that we are not
misled: we simply let off a kind of guilty steam. This too is
probably an inevitable, not a contingent, fact: it is easier to see
oneself as a naughty child who *knows* quite well what he has
done wrong, and accepts blame for it, than as one who is (as in
fact we usually are) very much in the dark about whether his
actions and attitudes are right or wrong. Guilt which is earthed
by having a clear target is easier to bear than a more free-
floating *Angst* and uncertainty; the most popular literature (at
least in our lazier moods) is that in which the heroes have no
general doubts of this kind, but require only or chiefly the
executive virtues (courage, loyalty, and so on).

Men are then to be seen as selfish only in a somewhat refined
or sophisticated sort of way: they are not self-seeking as cattle
or lions are self-seeking. They are systematically self-
deceiving, and unconsciously throw up a sort of screen or
proschema to cover the syllogisms by which they are in fact
guided. Their vision is distorted and their descriptions of the
world corrupted. Because of this, it is in general true to say
that they usually think that what they do is right, even when it
involves genocide, torture, deceit, injustice and the rest. Of
course (a) they *know* perfectly well that genocide, torture, etc.
are bad things, and (b) faced with them in the abstract (I mean,
shorn of all other possible descriptions) they often have the *will*
to avoid them. What happens is that they *describe them in some
other way*: genocide is a purification of the race, the torture

just a form of interrogation or inquisition, the deceit no more than white lies necessary for a greater good, the injustice – seen from a certain viewpoint – not really unjust after all. Wars could not be fought, nor persecutions accomplished, nor oppression continued, if it were not that men are permanently liable to invent and be persuaded by various ideologies, prejudices, question-begging descriptions and other kinds of rationalisations.

In this (admittedly rather desperate) sense men are rational and feel obliged to continue to be rational: they are not to be cured by non-rational methods (a hot poultice, a cold shower, a dose of will-power), nor yet by being given more or better straightforward factual information – as if they were straightforwardly *ignorant* and knew no better (as we might be ignorant of how to cure cancer). They need to be made to *see more clearly*. Hence it is at least possible for philosophy to intervene: possible, also, for a person to become sufficiently attached to the notion of truth in general and philosophical truth in particular for him to have some hope of emerging partially from this morass of autism. A great deal that Plato says about philosophy and philosophical training is relevant here, and it would be impertinent of me to repeat it. We need, however, a somewhat clearer idea of some of the escape-routes we may expect people to use. Given these immense difficulties with which the self is afflicted, we can see, I think, that men are necessarily driven to two devices, both of which ultimately serve the same purpose. If there is something wrong in or with oneself, one may either (i) *deny* it, thus keeping the self intact and trouble-free (or at least pretending that it is so), or (ii) *project* the trouble outside the self, with the same effect. These two moves (about which psychologists have written a great deal) can be seen as logically necessary: that is, an argument could be constructed to show that the concept marked by 'seeking to get rid of trouble in place X' can be logically explicated into 'denying the trouble' and 'relocating the trouble'.

In so far as it is not denied, on what will the trouble be projected? Here too some *a priori* considerations are helpful. As with children, there seems to be a natural developmental sequence. The first, because the easiest and least sophisticated, stage is one in which figures or phenomena are actually invented just to do the job of being suitable targets for projection. Fate, or stellar influence, or various kinds of god and demon, or some other largely imaginary features are made to bear the burdens we want them to bear. Before the advent of science men could happily believe in such things, for lack of any preventative scientific methodology; and even after science was firmly established in at least some societies, men can be found (not only within lunatic asylums) to have fantasies about germs, astrology, radio waves, the purity of blood and so forth. However, science puts some pressure to advance towards the second stage, which involves laying the blame on some actually existing thing that seems a suitable candidate. There are many such candidates, but two in particular claim our attention: (1) authority-figures or power-holders are chosen, for the obvious reason that a person with power may more plausibly be blamed than a person without it; and (2) aliens – that is, people sharply differentiated from ourselves and those like us by reason of their colour, race, creed, language or whatever – because aliens, whom *ex hypothesi* we know and understand less, are natural candidates for the possession of powers used for our harm.

A third state arises when men achieve at least a surface rationalism *vis-à-vis* human beings (in our culture, reasonably held to originate in the last two or three centuries). Rationalism of this kind – the idea, that is, of social science – tends to vitiate these second-stage targets for our projection: though, of course, they persist nevertheless alongside both the earlier targets of the first stage and these later ones. But the natural recipient for projection is now 'society' in general. That the meaning of 'society' is obscure of course helps, rather than hinders, the projection: the term sounds 'scientific' or 'sociological' enough to persuade the user that he is being rational, but it is vague enough for 'society' to entertain or sponsor almost any image we care to project. 'Society' determines us, cripples us, enchains us, forces us into 'roles' and 'classes', and so forth.

Marxist and post-Marxist movements (Women's Liberation, for instance) are fairly pure examples of this; and it is unsurprising that they have achieved a popularity which Freudianism (if, indeed, that term is even intelligible) has never come near having. It is very difficult to make any kind of *cause* out of

Freud's ideology precisely because it forbids projection: there is no one and nothing visible and overt against whom (which) to take up arms, as we may take up arms against the bosses, or 'the system'. Sci-disant Freudians have managed to form gangs only by a romantic misreading of Freud, whereby (for instance) much blame could be put on wicked parents, parsons and schoolmasters for 'repression' and progressive schools founded which were supposed to be free, in a Rousseauesque sort of way, from this imposed corruption. Even then the gang was a small one, consisting chiefly of a few intellectuals with sexual hang-ups, and bearing no comparison with the way that Marxist or some similar kind of sociological ideology has swept vast areas of the globe. Freud in fact brings us uncomfortably near to home, as uncomfortably as the classical Greek tragedians or St Augustine: what goes wrong is, in a strong if altered and still somewhat unclear sense, *our fault*. Our present obsession with 'society' was developmentally predictable, and could have been (perhaps in fact was) predicted by anyone who took the trouble to engage in a little philosophical sociology.

But of course not all forms of these devices are sociological or society-oriented: a deep-rooted fear of reason and preference for ideological commitment can take almost any form. Faiths, creeds, ideologies and emotional investments of various kinds come and go, and we cannot hope to cover all the ground; but perhaps one example (fairly typical and of fairly long standing) may be useful. This comes from an article by the director of an educational project in religious studies: I quote it because he is clear-headed enough to write clearly (Hulmes, 1975, pp. 33, 35, 37). He is challenging the idea that the approach in British universities "is very different . . . from that which is characteristic of a Marxist university, for example, where the principles of open enquiry are subordinated to the acceptance of a social theory and to a particular interpretation of the historical process. . . . It appears that only convinced – one may say, committed – Marxists are acceptable as teachers"; and himself says that

> . . . our discussion suggested that a man's religious commitment ought not to prejudice his professional commitment, in our case to the canons of liberal orthodoxy. This is to say, that no one is acceptable in a Western university who is not

committed to a detached and objective pursuit of truth. If this *is* the case, then I do not see how this situation differs in kind from that which exists in the Marxist university. In both cases, east and west, there is an ideological commitment which is in its own way exclusive. The difference between the two institutions is *not* that one is closed to new ideas and the other open.

But, of course, to extend 'ideological' so that it covers *any* kind of 'value' in this way just obscures the point: there is a significant difference between the person who says "You have got to believe such-and-such (Christianity, Marxism, environmentalism in biology, evolution, or whatever): we will not tolerate non-believers, and we will not have it questioned or its truth assessed in a detached and objective way and we do not welcome new ideas if they conflict with our ideology" and the person who says "No doubt we all have various beliefs but in *this* context we are concerned only with seeking truth and the procedures (being detached, objective and so on) that help to get it, and hence not only with substantive beliefs but with the methods, virtues, procedures, attitudes, etc. that may help to get at truth (e.g. being 'objective'), and we welcome any new ideas that may help." The one is not concerned with determining truth, but with preserving, publicising, or wallowing in some specific belief simply *taken* to be true; the other is, as the author says, 'committed to a detached and objective pursuit of truth'. If that is not a difference in kind, I do not know what is.

He continues

> My second point may be made by asking the question "What kind of *Christian* commitment is it which is prepared to subordinate personal and private insights to the demands of a professional and public commitment". The Christian is in a different position. Can he accept the professional constraints to which I have referred and remain committed to a faith which demands of him a *total* response in every part of life?

Here the word 'Christian' is brandished to make us feel that any and every feature of a Christian commitment ought to take precedence over other kinds of commitment: e.g., one supposes, if any such features or any 'personal and private in-

sights' clash with what is required by the academic pursuit and
dispensation of truth in a university, then the latter ought to
lose. But it is not a defining characteristic of 'Christian' (or
indeed 'religious' more generally) that Christian (religious)
pressures must always be treated as overriding. Some Soviet
biologists sold out on the rational procedures of biological
science for ideological reasons, but not all; and notoriously (or
famously) Christians have adopted all sorts of more or less
compromising or uncompromising postures in relation to various establishments.

Other passages suggest, what one might suspect already,
that the author does not have a sufficiently clear and differentiated concept of genuine *enquiry* and rational disagreement or
agreement to differ; or, if he has, does not trust it. Hence he
can write

> A society which considers it proper to preserve the right of
> each of us to dissent from the other, and of others in their
> turn equally to disagree about basic issues of life and death,
> simply because these differences *exist*, has scarcely begun to
> take seriously any of the rival world views. . . . I soon
> discover that I am committed to *one* set of beliefs and values,
> whereas my neighbour is committed to another, and thus to
> a very different course of *action*. In good faith (it is to be
> hoped) he and I are committed to conflicting and to possibly
> mutually destructive aims and ideals.

But anyone who sees the point of preserving the right to
dissent would say just the opposite: it is just because we *can* see
how seriously these rival views may disrupt our lives by civil
strife or international war that we insist on a rule whereby A
may disagree with B but may not persecute, torture or kill B
for his beliefs. Of course we could renege on such a rule
(indeed in moments of stress, as in Nazi Germany, or McCar-
thy's America, we do renege); but there are both logical and
practical arguments which persuade us of its merits. (Briefly,
the logical one is that we should not prescribe, in advance of
any particular views, that disagreements should be fought out
rather than negotiated: the practical or historical, that we seem
to save a lot of blood-shed and suffering by exchanging arguments rather than blows.)

That, of course, depends partly on the idea that we do own an allegiance to reason and argument as a means of progress and lessening our disagreement (only partly: even if we did not have this hope, discussion – even fruitless discussion – is better than war). Here again the author does not disappoint us, since he makes it quite clear that he thinks reason may be happily set aside in favour of a preferred ideology: quoting with approval John Donne, for whom

> there was a commitment which was prior even to the commitment to reason. This was a commitment to God, in whose service reason and other gifts besides were deployed . . . .

In other words, one may formulate and decide to give one's allegiance to quite a complex ideology (including sophisticated terms like 'God') before or 'prior' to bringing reason to bear on the matter. This ideology, thus non-rationally formulated, then dictates just how much reason one can use where (perhaps even what is to count as 'reason') and for what purposes. This is a very obvious example of cheating. Of course we all cheat: but not quite so obviously.

If we are interested in reason, our first job is to eschew ideology and be reasonable. It is on *procedural* principles of some kind that we ought to put our money. Some philosophers suffer, I think, from a kind of split in which 'formal' issues are distinguished from 'substantive' issues or 'matters of content'. The split, by separating off conceptual or logical points from the rest of our thinking and feeling, leaves us free to pursue our own 'values' or 'commitments' as we choose. Procedural or strategic principles would exercise a much-needed discipline over us. Part of the trouble is that we are still bewitched by the idea of 'right answers' (or else in rebellion against the whole idea of there being such things), and think backwards from there to the kinds of reasoning that seem to produce (or not to produce) them: thereby concentrating, defensively or aggressively, on certain very simple and obvious kinds of rational procedures which we wrongly take to be a full explication of what it is to be reasonable – on mathematical or scientific proof, for example. We might do better to start at the other end, by getting clear about what a reasonable man would look like, and what would count as a reasonable posture in the face of certain questions or conflicts: and from there move slowly towards, first, an understanding of the procedures we need, and secondly some tentative, revisable, and contestable outline of what truths these procedures seem to lead us towards.

The idea that one has first to know the right answer, or (more broadly) to have reached agreement about the desirability of a certain end-product, before one can say anything about what counts as conducting an enterprise well or reasonably, is doubly mistaken. First, there are some virtues which apply to all or almost all enterprises, some parts of what is meant by 'being reasonable' which are relevant to whatever we undertake; it would be hard to think of enterprises for which items like determination, conscientiousness, paying attention to the facts, elementary logic, open-mindedness and many others were not useful or essential. Secondly, we have some idea at least – perhaps a fairly clear idea – of qualities required for a certain enterprise in advance of that enterprise reaching its goal: we know, for instance, what counts as a good barrister independently of his winning particular law-suits, and what counts as a good scientist independently of his particular scientific discoveries. This is because we have some idea of the *methodology* of the enterprise: we know that barristers must argue clearly and incisively on points of law in front of judges and against opponents, that scientists must be imaginative in framing hypotheses and self-critical in testing them, and so forth. We know what the enterprise is about.

The phrase 'what the enterprise is about' points only in a very general direction; but in many cases it fits better than other phrases. Thus it might be appropriate sometimes to speak of the 'object', 'point' or 'purpose' of the enterprise, or to raise the question "What are we trying to produce or achieve here?" (for instance, in constructing motor cars or getting someone to pass an examination). At other times we may want to talk of the 'methodology' of the enterprise; particularly perhaps if it is a sophisticated form of rational enquiry, like science. But often we do not want to straitjacket the enterprise in that sort of way: no one, strictly speaking, should ask what the *methodology* of marriage ought to be, or even what marriage is *for*: that may degrade it by giving it in advance the status of a means to an end, which it may not be. But it is very much in order to ask what marriage is *about*. In trying to answer such a question, we should talk about the form of life marked by 'marriage', in such a way that the enquirer came to understand what it was like: and in doing this, we could not avoid some mention of the difficulties and obstacles, the characteristic mistakes and successes, and the virtues and vices which figure in it. We should speak of separation and divorce, give and take, living in each other's pocket and *egoisme à deux*, faithfulness and disloyalty, sharing and sympathising, jealousy and sacrifice, and many other things.

It might be said: "But surely the only test of whether a particular methodology is appropriate is whether or not it produces right answers: so we have to start by knowing some 'absolutely right' (true, etc.) answers, and if we have no reason to believe in such then we have no reason to believe in the methodology." Any plausibility there is in this derives from the fact that *if* the methodology is appropriate, then it *will* produce some right answers. Viewed from a certain aspect, that might be taken as a loose conceptual point: right answers are characteristically generated by what is a rational approach to the problem. Being serious or rational, we might say, has a *point*: it is not just an aesthetic posture. But we would not withdraw terms like 'serious' or 'rational' in all cases even if no right answers were generated, because they are not *defined* by such generation: it is conceivable, for instance, that a clairvoyant or crystal-gazer produced some correct predictions, and that scientists did not, in a certain field of enquiry – but that would not be sufficient to make us believe that crystal-gazing was a more reasonable approach to the field than science was.

The connections really work in a reverse direction: in a sense, and in some enquiries in every sense, what counts as a right answer is whatever answer is generated by the appropriate methodology. In mathematics, for instance, we work on the basis of certain rules or axioms (including rules of procedure), and the right answer is identified by applying those rules correctly. In aesthetics, however impossibly thorny this area may be, it is not ridiculous to say (as Aristotle often does) that things are as they appear to the reasonable and serious man: it is possible to identify a good critic without first being entirely clear about what ways there are of proving this or that piece of art or literature to be good. Perhaps there are no such ways; or perhaps they cannot be logically divorced from the notion of an ideal observer. Even morality, or some aspects of morality, may work like this.

The enterprise which we might entitle 'truth-seeking', 'using one's reason', 'trying to get things right', or whatever, like any other enterprise (or thing), is represented under various descriptions or by various concepts and words. These of course carry certain implications with them: there are things which we can or cannot consistently or intelligibly say in connection with them. We cannot say, for instance, "I am seeking the true facts of the case, but really what one counts as a fact is entirely arbitrary, or a matter of personal decision, or a matter of what my culture counts as a fact"; or "I am searching for the truth, but truth is something which I can create myself"; or "I am trying to get the right answer, but there is really no such thing as 'the right answer'." Such a speaker may be wanting to say something, perhaps various things: but not those things, since the propositions as they stand have no sense.

Amongst the candidates for what such speakers may be wanting to say are: (1) that individuals and whole cultures are often mistaken in what they *call* true, reasonable, etc.; (2) that the search for truth takes place against, within, and as a result of a certain social background; (3) that what counts as true, reasonable, etc. is a function of a certain predetermined set of rules made by men. Of these, (1) is correct, and acknowledges the non-relativity of truth (if an individual or culture can be mistaken, it can also be right); (2) is boringly obvious; and only (3) is of any serious interest. What counts as correct, however, is never *wholly* a function of the rules, except in cases where the form of life is totally insulated from the irruptions of the real world, as in games and (perhaps) mathematics. In all other cases, whilst the rules determine what is to count as a fact – in effect, what counts as relevant experience – they do not determine what actually *is* a fact. We set up scientific experiments, called 'scientific' because they are designed to trap certain things (the movements of bodies, etc.) and not other things (their beauty, sacredness, etc.): but the design does not yield this particular movement rather than that. (Otherwise they would not be experiments.) The real world participates. Moreover, the rules we set up for particular purposes are not arbitrary: if one is serious in wanting to predict the physical world, science (rather than astrology) becomes necessary.

They are man-made: but man can make then well or badly –
that is, more or less sensibly in relation to what sort of grip he
wants to have on the real world.

Being reasonable in general, and doing philosophy in a practical and useful way in particular, are then matters of general
posture or *attitude*: not matters of being in possession of some
kind of revealed truth. We are dealing here, not with particular
propositions, but with principles and procedures. In the educational world, and perhaps in our own and other societies more
generally, there seems to be a strong climate of opinion against
making principles of reason explicit and trying to get our pupils
to adopt them, even when we are tolerably clear what the
principles are. Why this climate exists is not a philosophical
enquiry: but it partly accounts for the lack of much visible or
clear-cut philosophical and other kinds of education in practice. Yet much practical work that *is* done implicitly relies on
such principles: the mere practice of rational debate about
moral issues for instance, now fairly wide-spread, incorporates
a whole set of principles and values which, if made explicit and
pressed home, might turn out to be much the same as those
that many now stigmatise under the title of 'liberal ideology'. I
am thinking of such things as tolerance, equality of status in the
debate, the pursuit of insight, clarity in the use of words, and at
least (or so I hope) the search for what counts as relevant
evidence or good grounds. Without all these and more the
debate could hardly survive, let alone flourish. It would not be
too difficult to show that these were in fact principles of reason
or of any serious search for truth, not any kind of ideology. Of
course someone who thinks – if such a thought is coherent –
that reason and truth are themselves a function of ideological
outlook would not be persuaded; but for those of us who
believe that we can do more than just cling to our ideologies or
foist them on other people had better be as clear as possible
about just what principles and procedures we are willing to
defend.

It is worth all our whiles to reflect, psychologically rather
than logically, on the feelings which underlie much of these
disputes. We have perhaps the fantasy that 'reason' (and not
only that, but such connected notions as 'truth', 'mental

health', 'good government' and a host of others) means what someone else says it means. Then either we defer to this supposed authority or – much more common in our century – we redistribute the authority to each individual, so as to make him (or his culture) the judge of his own case, and start talking about 'autonomy' and 'democracy'. I am myself guiltily conscious of having moved, and no doubt still moving, between the two poles of this fantasy, which is an obvious and ultimately boring echo of almost everyone's childhood: and I do not suppose that I am the only sinner. Much blood, as well as ink, would be saved if we had a better appreciation of just why we feel impelled to say what we do on those matters: such appreciation might then lead us to consider the meanings of words, and a proper strategy for the selection of concepts, in their own right. Thus people often say things like "You're talking as if there were an absolute set of values laid down by (or laid up in) heaven, some absolute authority, but there's not." No: *they* are talking as if that were so. They can conceive of an absolute authority *or* of total arbitrariness, but find it hard to conceive of being reasonable about things – perhaps through lack of practice in childhood.

I incline to think, indeed, that a certain type of personal experience is required if one is to escape fully from these chains: perhaps the experience of love or taking pleasure in some kind of work – intellectual or other – which clearly has authoritative standards of success, but where one does not feel that these standards are unfairly imposed or questionable. In practical education that is perhaps only too rare an experience for pupils; and of course there is a vicious circle here, since some people have a vested interest in seeing any standards as ('by definition') tyrannical (just as others will see any rules as worthy of obedience). This distinctly Sartrean sort of isolation, which more or less consciously denies the importance or the reality of primary affection, fraternity, or love, may make it ultimately impossible to do any serious philosophical business at all: indeed my view is that philosophy is logically, not just empirically, dependent on attitudes and social contexts of this kind, which are always in short supply. Those philosophers who wish to cut ice in the outside world would do well to pursue this enquiry further than I have done.

A Practical Postscript

I have tried above all to show in this book that philosophy can have immense *practical* force and value in human life. But – perhaps for reasons given in the last two chapters, where we discussed our resistances to philosophy in particular and reason in general – it is clear that this view of philosophy is not properly institutionalised or put into practice. Hence the philosopher may fairly be asked some question of the general form "Assuming you are right about philosophy, what do you recommend should be *done* about it?"

The philosopher as such can hardly be expected to say very much about this, since the question is largely an empirical one. It is a matter of political (sociological, psychological, etc.) fact and theory whether this or that practical move is likely to put philosophy more effectively on the map in this or that society at this or that particular time; and the answers to the question will clearly vary with local conditions. Nevertheless, there are certain rather broad or general points – points which might still be fairly called 'practical' – which can be made here, and which need making if philosophy is ever to play the part which it ought to play. I will simply list these in order, being only too aware that very much more needs to be said about them all.

(1) The first point is that philosophy requires a good deal more publicity than it actually gets (even in societies where philosophy is widely practised). At the same time, of course, it also requires explanation: people need to know not just that there is such a thing, but what sort of thing it is (that is why I have written this book). But without effective publicity their attention is not likely to be caught, and they are not likely to get even as far as listening to any explanation. The comparatively large amount of publicity given to sociology, psychology and other disciplines is striking: this imbalance has to be

151

redressed. Philosophers must fight for their share of the market.

(2) More importantly, everyone needs to be taught some philosophy (or, better, what philosophy is and how to do it) in school and in higher education. On the view taken in this book, philosophy is not an option which some people may take up for their own interest or amusement, but a vital piece of equipment for every person – as vital as a mastery of their native language, or elementary mathematics, or anything else. There is no reason to disbelieve, and plenty of reasons to believe, that even quite young children can do philosophy; certainly all should have adequate experience of it before their education is over. Philosophers must fight for their share of the curriculum.

(3) Philosophy is of course important for the life of each individual, but its lack may be thought to become particularly obvious in those collective enterprises which are intimately connected with concepts and values. Almost all human and non-technical enterprises are of this kind: marriage and friendship, education, social work, church ministry, mental health, politics and many others. Unless such enterprises are in some reasonable degree controlled, or at the very least monitored, by philosophers they will inevitably go badly wrong (as many of them have in fact very obviously gone wrong). In most societies (to speak broadly) it is the politician, the sociologist, the bureaucrat or some other kind of expert who wields most of the power or is most attended to. Here is another imbalance to be redressed: philosophers must fight for their share of control in these enterprises.

Points like these need to be made (and something needs to be done about them), but are of course bound to seem naive in the light of various obstacles that at once spring to mind – not only the surface obstacles of scarce finance and resources, competition from other disciplines, institutional hostility to philosophy, etc. but also the more deep-rooted resistances mentioned in previous chapters. Even so, it is possible for us to move too quickly from a proper realism to an improper despair: something can in fact be done, and done without too much difficulty, if philosophers (by which term I include anyone who wishes to promote the cause of philosophy) are willing to do it.

That, however, seems to be a very big 'if'. It ought to be seen as surprising and scandalous that philosophers – some of whom, in the UK and other societies, hold eminent positions and have considerable influence both socially and financially – have made so little effort to promote their subject in a practical way. Some may regard such promotion as virtually impossible, taking the view that we are up against invincible ignorance. Others may think it in some way improper, degrading to the subject, to hire a good advertising or public-relations agent, or to use any but the most stringently rational and non-emotive methods to advance the cause of philosophy. Others again may simply not be very interested – and it is, in fact an important question whether the missionary and pragmatic zeal required for selling philosophy can co-exist, in the same person, with the patience and scholarship required for doing it well. I do not – not, at least, without further research – wish to accuse my colleagues in the profession of moral slackness. At the same time there does seem to be some sort of conceptual connection between thinking philosophy important for all men and doing something to promote it; and I end with the hope that all who think it important will do rather more than they have done hitherto.

References

Austin, Jean (1973) 'Teaching Moral Philosophy', in A. Montefiore (ed.), *Philosophy and Personal Relations* (London: Routledge).

Austin, J. L. (1961) *Philosophical Papers* (Oxford University Press).

Ayer, A. J. (1936) *Language, Truth and Logic* (London: Macmillan).

Bambrough, R. (1967) 'Plato's Political Analogies', in R. Bambrough (ed.), *Plato, Popper and Politics* (Cambridge: Heffer).

Dearden, R. F. (1968) *The Philosophy of Primary Education* (London: Routledge).

Dearden, R. F., Hirst, P. H. and Peters, R. S. (eds) (1972) *Education and the Development of Reason* (London: Routledge).

Frege, G. (1950) *The Foundations of Arithmetic*, trans. J. L. Austin (Oxford University Press).

Hare, R. M. (1963) *Freedom and Reason* (Oxford University Press).

—— (1970) General introduction to *The Dialogues of Plato* (London: Sphere).

—— (1971) *Essays on Philosophical Method* (London: Macmillan).

—— (1972) *Applications of Moral Philosophy* (London: Macmillan).

—— (1976) 'Ethical Theory and Utilitarianism', in H. D. Lewis (ed.), *Contemporary British Philosophy* (London: Allen & Unwin).

Hartnett, A. and Naish, M. (1976) *Theory and the Practice of Education* (London: Heinemann).

Hirst, P. H. and Peters, R. S. (1970) *The Logic of Education* (London: Routledge).

Hirst, P. H. (1974) *Knowledge and the Curriculum* (London: Routledge).

Hospers, J. (1956) *Introduction to Philosophical Analysis* (London: Routledge).

Hulmes, E. (1975) 'The Problem of Commitment', in *The Worcester Papers* (Oxford: Farmington Institute).

Gallie, W. B. (1956) 'Essentially Contested Concepts', in *Proceedings of the Aristotelian Society*, vol. 60, pp. 167–98.

—— (1964) *Philosophy and the Historical Understanding* (London: Chatto & Windus).

Lipman, M. (1977) *Philosophy in the Classroom* (Montclair State College, New Jersey: Institute for the Advancement of Philosophy for Children).

Lucas, J. (1966) *Principles of Politics* (Oxford University Press).
Macintyre, A. (1964) 'Is Understanding Religion Compatible with Believing?', in J. Hick (ed.), *Faith and the Philosophers* (London: Macmillan).
—— (1966) *A Short History of Ethics* (London: Macmillan).
Magee, B. (ed.) (1971) *Modern British Philosophy* (London: Secker & Warburg.
—— (ed.) (1978) *Men of Ideas* (London: BBC).
Montefiore, A. (1979) 'Philosophy and Moral (and Political) Education', in *Journal of Philosophy of Education*, vol. 13.
Peters, R. S. (1966) *Ethics and Education* (London: Allen & Unwin).
Quinton, A. (1973) *The Nature of Things* (London: Routledge).
—— (1975) 'Has Man an Essence?', in R. S. Peters (ed.), *Nature and Conduct* (London: Macmillan).
Ryan, A. (1974) 'An Essentially Contested Concept', in *The Times Higher Educational Supplement*, 1 Feb.
Ryle, G. (ed.) (1956) *The Revolution in Philosophy* (London: Macmillan).
—— (1963) 'Ordinary Language', in C. Caton (ed.), *Philosophy and Ordinary Language* (Urbana: University of Illinois Press).
Strawson, P. F. (1962) *Freedom and Resentment* (Oxford University Press).
—— (ed.) (1967) *Philosophical Logic* (Oxford University Press).
Toulmin, S. (1972) *Human Understanding* (Oxford University Press).
Urmson, J. (1969) 'Austin's Philosophy', in K. Fann (ed.), *Symposium on J. L. Austin* (London: Routledge).
Warnock, G. J. (1975) 'Kant and Anthropology', in R. S. Peters (ed.), *Nature and Conduct* (London: Macmillan).
Winch, P. (1972) 'Nature and Convention', in his *Ethics and Action* (London: Routledge).
Wilson, J. (1956) *Language and the Pursuit of Truth* (Cambridge University Press).
—— (1963) *Thinking with Concepts* (Cambridge University Press).
—— (1968) *Philosophy* (London: Heinemann).
—— (1971a) *Education in Religion and the Emotions* (London: Heinemann).
—— (1971b) *Practical Methods of Moral Education* (London: Heinemann).
—— (1972) *Philosophy and Educational Research* (Slough, Bucks: National Foundation of Educational Research).
—— (1977) *Philosophy and Practical Education* (London: Routledge).
—— (1979a) *Preface to the Philosophy of Education* (London: Routledge).

—— (1979b) *Fantasy and Common Sense in Education* (Oxford: Martin Robertson).

—— (1980) *Love, Sex and Feminism* (New York: Praeger).

Suggestions for Introductory Reading

For the reader who is not familiar with modern philosophy, I suggest (tentatively):

1. for a general survey of the field, Magee (1971) and (1978), and Ryle (1956);
2. for introductions to philosophical method, Wilson (1963), Hospers (1956), and Hare (1971);
3. for collections of important short articles on various branches of philosophy, the series *Oxford Readings in Philosophy*, general editor, G. J. Warnock (Oxford University Press).

Index

Ambiguity, 54
Analytic truth, 9ff.
Aristotle, 57
Austin, J. L., 9, 12, 37ff.
Austin, Jean, 105ff.
Authority, 87
Autism, 10, 102ff., 137

Bambrough, J., 31
Berlin, I., 28ff.

Categorisation, 56ff.
Christianity, 143ff.
Coherence, 15
Concepts, nature, of, 41ff.
Concepts and history, 49
Conceptual analysis, 2ff.
Conceptual truths, 15, 19ff.
Contestable concepts, 41ff.
Convention, 21ff.

Dearden, R. F., 90
Definitions, 47
Denial, 140

Education, 48ff.
Elites, 99

Fact and value, 27ff.
Fantasy, 123ff.
Forms of knowledge, 88ff.
Frege, G., 41, 49
Freud, S., 141ff.

Gallie, W., 46ff., 55
Grice, P., 9
Guilt, 139

Hare, R. M., 22ff., 30, 32, 100

Hart, H., 69, 85
Hartnett, A., 47ff., 52
Hirst, P. H., 44, 82, 86, 88ff.
Hulmes, E., 142ff.

Ideology, vii, 1, 3, 9, 10, 39, 58,
    77, 103, 111, 143
Institutions, 87
Integrity, 106
Introductions to philosophy, 131

Kant, I., 63ff., 72

Linguistics, 75ff.
Lipman, M., 10
Lucas, J., 69, 87

Mackintyre, A., 78, 93
Magee, B., 2, 27ff.
Montefiore, A., 57
Morality, 28ff., 78

Naish, M., 47ff., 52

Ordinary language, 9, 11, 36ff.

Passion, 132
People, 77ff.
Peters, R. S., 44, 48, 81, 85ff.
Philosophy and expertise, 27ff.; and
    society, 106ff.
'Philosophy of Life', 2
Plato, 10, 55, 57, 97, 99, 100, 107,
    108, 122
Preconditions for philosophy, 121ff.
Promotion of philosophy, 152
Psychotherapy, 121ff.

Quine, W., 9
Quinton, A., 21, 61

Racial prejudice, 97ff.
Rationality, 68ff.
Reasonableness, 132ff.
Relativism, 148
Research, 127ff.
Right answers, 146ff.
Ryan, A., 48
Ryle, G., 38, 103, 107, 109

Science, 93
Social work, 114
'Society', 141
Sociology, 115, 122
Spontaneity, 103
Strawson, P., 60, 63ff., 80, 85

Teacher–pupil relationships, 105
Teaching Philosophy (journal), 5, 8
Theory, 112ff.
Toulmin, S., 63ff.
Trust, 125ff.
Truth, 14ff.

Urmson, J., 37

Virtue, 33ff.

Warnock, G., 67ff.
Williams, B., 2, 49
Winch, P., 34
Wittgenstein, L., 121